Young CHEFS

A Dorling Kindersley Book

DK

LONDON, NEW YORK,
MELBOURNE, MUNICH, and DELHI

Senior Editor Charis Bhagianathan
Assistant Art Editor Astha Singh
Photographers Will Heap, Dave King,
Pravin Pol, Ganesh Shedge, Howard Shooter,
Dayakar Soma, Michael Swamy
Food Stylist Parul Pratap Shirazi
Illustrator Arun Pottirayil
Proofreaders Divya Chandhok, Medha Gupta
DTP Designers Nandkishor Acharya,
Dheeraj Singh
Pre-production Manager Narender Kumar
Production Manager Pankaj Sharma
Deputy Managing Editor Alka Ranjan
Consultant Art Director Shefali Upadhyay
General Manager Production Ajay Joshi
Vice President Production Subhasis Ganguli
Managing Director Aparna Sharma

Cover image Munish Byala, with special thanks
to Avani Mehra and Ankush Mehra

First published in India in 2013
by Dorling Kindersley Publishing Private Ltd,
8, Local Shopping Centre, Panchsheel Park,
New Delhi 110017, India

A CIP catalogue record for this book is available
from the British Library

ISBN 978-1-40934-823-8

Printed and bound in New Delhi
by Thomson Press India Ltd.

Discover more at
www.dk.com

CONTENTS

INTRODUCTION

To my dearest little chef,

With great pride and love, I present to you a cookbook designed especially for the enthusiastic chef in you. As a grown-up I can vouch that as you grow older, the fondest memories that you will carry will be of aromas and flavours of the warm comforting mealtimes spent at your family table, surrounded by your loved ones.

I grew up learning to cook as my grandmother's little kitchen helper. I ran to her kitchen at every opportunity I got, fascinated with all the smells and actions in the kitchen: rolling, baking, chopping, stirring, and whisking.

Let me tell you about the very first time I learned to roll bread. When I was a child, growing up in Amritsar, my mom took me to the Golden Temple to offer prayers and to eat at the *langar*, or the community kitchen. As we sat in the same line with everybody to share the food together, I noticed the women in the kitchen rolling the breads and chanting *wahe guru*. Watching my fascination, an elderly lady called me to her side and gave me her rolling pin. Feeling quite confident of myself, I set out with maximum concentration to roll what I was sure would be a perfect *roti*.

I have yet to figure how to describe the shape of that first *roti* – not sure which country's map it resembled. Nonetheless, I proudly served my first bread to my mother, who cherishes the memory till today.

It is said "you are what you eat". Preparing food yourself will teach you about healthy eating, balanced diet, and fresh ingredients. As a child I was sometimes picky about eating my greens and veggies. My grandmother found a great solution

for my pickiness. She would call me to her kitchen table and ask me to watch and help with dinner. As I worked by her side, shelling peas and washing spinach, she explained how tasty and nutritious the veggies were for me. Finally when the dish was ready, I was so proud to have helped cook it that not only did I eat it with relish, I made sure my brother and sister ate it too.

If the kitchen scares you, just remember the greatest chefs were all once little chefs like yourself – they all had to learn how to crack an egg, measure ingredients, and other skills that you will perfect in time with practice, patience, and persistence. Recipes in this book are a starting point. If you don't like an ingredient, give it a miss or try another item you'd much rather have.

As you don your apron and chef hat and head to the kitchen, I hope this book will be the beginning of a long and happy journey of delicious creations.

So, here's to the future Michelin-star chef!

Vikas Khanna

For my nieces Ojasvi and Saumya Khanna: Thank you for bringing new light in my life every day. You are my most treasured "Young Chefs"!

GETTING STARTED

Transforming a set of ingredients into something new is not only magical but is a great life skill. This book gives you ideas to try new recipes for breakfast, lunch box, main meals, and sweet treats. Whether you want to fry an egg, bake cookies, or concoct something more complicated, such as chicken tikka masala, just follow the recipe's easy steps.

THINGS TO REMEMBER

1. Read a recipe all the way through before you start.
2. Wash your hands, put on an apron and tie back your hair.
3. Make sure you have all the ingredients and equipment before you begin a recipe.

KEY TO SYMBOLS USED IN THE RECIPES

How many people the dish serves, or how many portions it makes.

Preparation time, including chilling, freezing, and marinating.

Cooking time
A few recipes, such as the salads, don't have this symbol.

SAFETY IN THE KITCHEN

Ask an adult to help when you see this symbol. Take extra care because hot ovens, hobs, or sharp implements, such as knives are involved.

WEIGHTS AND MEASUREMENTS

Carefully weigh out the ingredients before you start a recipe. Use measuring spoons, weighing scales, and a measuring jug as necessary. Below are the full names for measurements and their abbreviations.

METRIC MEASURES
g = gram
ml = millilitre

IMPERIAL MEASURES
oz = ounce
lb = pound
fl oz = fluid ounce

SPOON MEASURES
tsp = teaspoon
tbsp = tablespoon

KITCHEN HYGIENE

When you're in the kitchen, follow these important rules to keep the germs in check.

- Always wash your hands before you start any recipe.

- Wash all fruit and vegetables.

- Use separate chopping boards for meat and vegetables.

- Keep your cooking area clean and have a cloth handy to mop up any spillages.

- Store raw and cooked food separately.

- Keep meat and fish in the fridge until you need them and always take care to cook them properly.

- Wash your hands after handling raw eggs or raw meat.

- Always check the use-by date on all ingredients.

- Discard leftover marinade that has been used to soak meat in.

HEALTHY EATING

You need to eat a balanced diet made up of a variety of different foods, so that you can grow, stay healthy, and have lots of energy for life.

FRUIT AND VEGETABLES

Your body can get important vitamins and minerals, as well as fibre, from fruit and vegetables. Aim to eat about five different portions of these a day. It's useful to think of a portion as roughly equal to the amount you can hold in one hand – such as an apple, a small bunch of grapes, two broccoli florets, or a bowl of salad.

STARCHY FOODS

Bread, cereals, rice, pasta, and potatoes are all starchy foods, also known as carbohydrates. These foods give you energy and should form a part of every meal – whether it's poha for breakfast, a sandwich lunch, or a pasta dish for dinner. Many starchy foods come in wholegrain varieties, which are healthier for you as they contain more vitamins, minerals, and fibre, as compared to the refined white versions.

PROTEIN

This type of food is made from amino acids, chemicals that work all over your body to keep you active and strong. We get protein from both animal and plant sources – meat, fish, nuts and seeds, beans, and dairy produce. It's healthy to eat a variety of these.

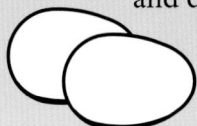

DAIRY PRODUCE

As well as being a source of protein, dairy produce provides valuable vitamins (vitamins A, B12, and D) and minerals (such as calcium). Dairy produce includes milk, yogurt, cheese, butter, cream, crème fraîche, and paneer. If you're not keen on dairy, then you can get these nutrients in other foods, such as soy milk, tofu, and baked beans.

FATS AND SUGARS

Everyone needs fat for energy and for their bodies to work properly, it's just that it has to be the right type of fat. Fats also help you absorb vitamins and provide essential fatty acids, such as omega-3 and omega-6. Healthy fats (known as polyunsaturated or monounsaturated) are found in vegetable oils, such as sesame, sunflower, soy, and olive, as well as in nuts, seeds, avocados, and oily fish, such as mackerel and salmon. Avoid eating saturated and trans fats (mostly in processed foods).

SUGARY FOODS AND SALT

Sugar gives you energy and it makes biscuits and cakes taste sweet. Eating too much sugar, though, can lead to mood swings, tooth decay, and obesity. Too much salt is linked with health problems. Avoid very salty snacks and adding too much salt to your cooking.

COOKING TOOLS

You need to use the right tools for each step. Most kitchens are equipped with the majority of these tools. Remember to be extra careful when using equipment that is sharp or uses electricity to power it. An adult should always supervise you while you're in the kitchen.

Whisk

Kitchen scissors

Pizza cutter

Fork

Spatula

Peelers

Wooden spoons

Basting brush

Large spoon

Sharp knife

Table knife

Spoons

Spaghetti claw

Sandwich cake tin

Baking trays

Loaf tin

Non-stick muffin tin

Pizza tray

Cutting boards

Cooling rack

Plastic container

Stock pot

Large bowl

Glass bowls

Small bowls

Colander

Milk pan

Square cake tin

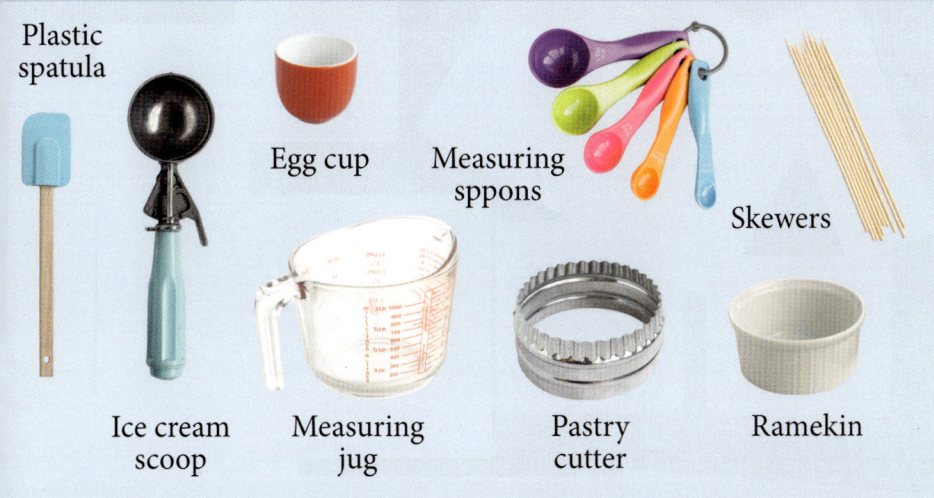

Food processor

Glass jar

Electric whisk

Masher

Food blender

Piping bag and nozzles

Chopping board

These are some of the tools typically used in an Indian kitchen.

Plastic spatula

Egg cup

Measuring sppons

Skewers

Ice cream scoop

Measuring jug

Pastry cutter

Ramekin

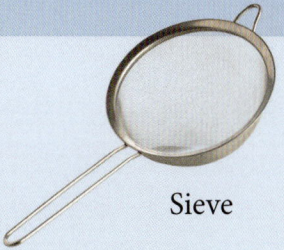
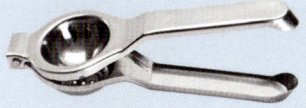

Slotted spoon

Sieve

Lemon crusher

Cookie cutters

Lasagne dish

Baking parchment

Oven dish

Ceramic flan dish

Cling film

Foil

Grater

Serving spoon

Ladle

Mortar and pestle

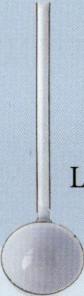

Rolling pin

Small casserole dish

Saucepan with lid

Glass jugs

Frying pan

Griddle pan

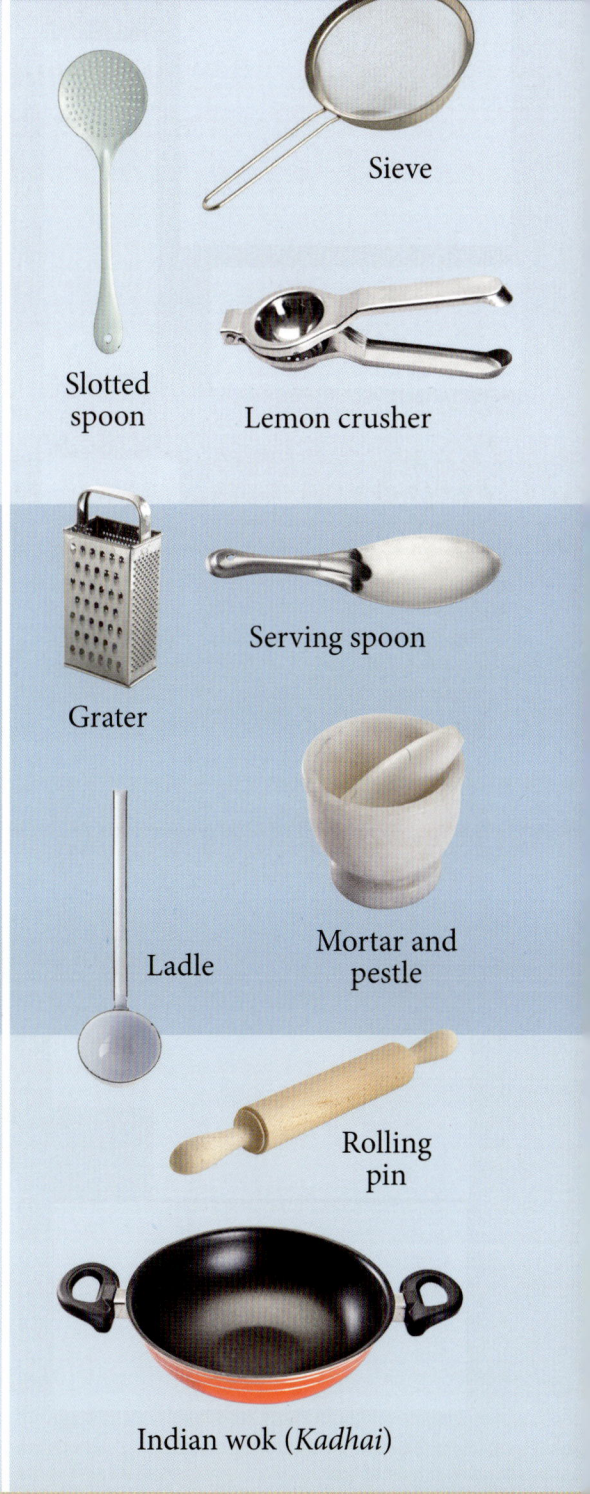

Indian wok (*Kadhai*)

WAYS TO COOK

Some foods are best cooked at low heat for a long time, while others respond best to a fast blast of heat. The different techniques shown below are used in different recipes to bring out the best flavours and textures of a dish.

BOIL

With the heat turned up high, a liquid will bubble vigorously when boiling.

SIMMER

With the heat on low, a mixture will bubble gently when simmering.

FRY

Drizzle some oil into a wide pan to fry food; it's also known as sautéing.

STIR-FRY

On a high heat and using oil, stir-frying cooks food fast and needs lots of stirring.

GRILL

With the heat coming from above, you need to turn food during grilling.

GRIDDLE

On high heat, a griddle pan's ridges put smoky stripes on the food.

BAKE

Cooking food in an oven is baking. Bread, biscuits, cakes, and pies are baked.

ROAST

Cooking meat, fish, or vegetables in the oven is known as roasting.

STEAM

Placing food above boiling water uses the steam to cook it.

DRY-ROASTING

Browning in a pan without oil is called dry-roasting.

DEEP-FRY

Completely immersing food in hot oil is known as deep-frying.

BBQ

Food can be roasted or grilled on a BBQ using heat from charcoal.

PREPARING INGREDIENTS

Before you start cooking you'll need to get all your ingredients ready. Depending on your recipe, you may have a lot of prep or very little to do.

DICE

To dice an onion, first slice it (while keeping it together) and then slice it at right angles to create small squares or dice. For a courgette, first cut into chunky sticks and then cut across these to make dice.

CHOP

Claw Hold the food using a "claw" shape to keep fingers clear of the knife.

Bridge Form a bridge between thumb and finger and cut beneath the bridge.

PEEL

Whatever you're peeling, hold the food in one hand and peel away from your body. Carrots are easily peeled from top to bottom, but apples can be peeled in one beautiful spiral – with practice. And watch out for your fingers, peelers are sharp.

GRATE

As the food passes over the grater's teeth, slithers are forced through.

MASH

Cooked root vegetables can be pushed through a masher until smooth.

Before   **After**

MAKE BREADCRUMBS

It's quickest done in a food processor. Tear pieces of dried-out bread into the bowl, pop the lid on, and whizz until crumbed. Or, you could grate chunks of the bread instead.

OTHER USEFUL TERMS

• **Toast** to make a food, such as bread or nuts, crisp, hot, and brown (see page 39)

• **Purée** a thick pulp of vegetables or fruit blended until smooth in a liquidizer or pushed through a sieve (see page 70)

• **Marinate** to mix food with a combination of oil, wine, or vinegar with herbs or spices to add flavour (see pages 90–91)

• **Blend** to mix together so you can't see any of the individual ingredients (see pages 103)

• **Knock back** bash out the excess air when bread dough has risen, before letting it prove (see pages 13, 36)

• **Drizzle** pouring a little stream of liquid, such as olive oil, in tiny drops (see page 68)

• **Season** adding salt and pepper

• **Toss** mix some dry ingredients in some wet ingredients, such as lettuce leaves in salad dressing or pasta shapes in a sauce (see page 44)

• **Reduce to thicken** heating a sauce gently until some of its water is lost (as steam) and the amount of sauce becomes less (see page 35)

• **Baste** to coat food with meat juice, a marinade or butter, while cooking (see page 83)

WAYS TO BAKE

To get cakes to rise, make light meringue, and perfect your pastry and biscuits, there are certain techniques in baking that you'll need to master. Once you know what's what you'll be a baking expert!

SIFT

Shaking flour or icing sugar through a sieve gets rid of lumps and adds air.

FOLD

1. Use a spatula to gently mix while keeping the air in the mixture.

2. Go around the edge of the bowl and then "cut" across, lifting as you go.

BEAT

Make a smooth, airy mixture by working fast with a wooden spoon.

SEPARATE AN EGG

1. Break the shell: tap the egg on the side of the bowl and open up.

2. Transfer the yolk from one shell to the other over a bowl; put the yolk in another bowl.

WHISK EGG WHITES

1. Mix in a lot of air into a mixture using an electric or a handheld whisk.

2. The mixture should be stiff; if you overwhisk, the mixture will collapse.

RUB IN

1. Many recipes mix fat (diced butter) and flour using this method.

2. Using your fingertips, pick up the mixture, break up the lumps, and let it fall.

3. Keep rubbing your thumb along your fingertips. To check you've got rid of all the lumps of butter, shake the bowl and any lumps will pop up to the surface.

MAKE A PIPING BAG

1. Carefully cut a square of baking parchment or greaseproof paper.
2. Fold the paper round on itself to form a cone with a pointy end. Tape in place.

3. Snip off the end of the cone for the icing or cream to come out: for a fine line, use a tiny cut; cut higher up the cone for a chunky line.

CREAM

1. When mixing butter and sugar together, use butter that's been left to soften at room temperature.
2. Cut the butter into pieces.

3. Using an electric whisk or a wooden spoon, beat the butter and sugar together until it's paler in colour, light, and fluffy.

HOW TO MAKE PIZZA DOUGH

1. Sift 500g (1lb 2oz) flour into a bowl and add 7g sachet of dried yeast and salt. Make a well in the centre, then slowly add 200ml (7fl oz) warm water.

2. Mix with a wooden spoon until it comes together and then add 4 tablespoons of olive oil and continue to mix until it forms a soft dough.

3. Knead firmly using the heel of your hand, folding the dough over as you go. Do this until the dough becomes soft and spongy.

4. Put the dough in a bowl, cover with cling film, and leave in a warm place for 30–40 minutes or until the dough has doubled in size.

5. Put the dough on a floured surface, and knead with your knuckles to knock out the air. Fold the dough over and knead again. It will become elastic and stretchy.

6. Divide the dough into four balls. Using a rolling pin, roll a ball out on a floured surface until it's about 1cm (½in) thick.

BREAKFAST BITES

INGREDIENTS

- 4 large eggs
- 240ml (8fl oz) milk
- ¼ tsp ground cinnamon
- 4 slices thick white bread, cut into triangles
- 2 tbsp sunflower oil
- 100g (3½oz) blueberries
- maple syrup, to serve

TOOLS

- whisk
- mixing bowl
- shallow dish
- frying pan and spatula

EGGY BREAD

Popular around the world, this dish is eaten in Portugal at Christmas and in Spain and Brazil at Easter.

Serves 2 | Prep 10 mins | Cook 10 mins

1 Crack the eggs into a mixing bowl. Add the milk and cinnamon, and whisk together.

2 Pour the mixture into a shallow dish. Soak the bread (for about 30 seconds) in the mixture.

3 Heat half a tablespoon of the oil in a frying pan on low heat. Place 2 triangles in the pan.

4 Fry the triangles on both sides until golden. Repeat steps 3 and 4 for the remaining bread triangles.

5 Serve the eggy bread warm, with blueberries and maple syrup, or try it with butter and jam.

FOUR WAYS WITH EGGS

Try these classic ways to cook an egg.

1

BOILED EGG

Boiled eggs are easy to make. How do you like your boiled egg? You can have it soft-, medium-, or hard-boiled.

INGREDIENTS

This recipe is for 1 person. It takes 2 minutes to prepare and 4-8 minutes to cook.

- 1 egg
- 1 slice of toast, buttered

METHOD

- Fill a small saucepan with water and use a slotted spoon to lower one egg into it. Ask an adult to boil the water.

- When the water has boiled, lower the temperature and let it simmer. Follow these cooking times:

soft-boiled 4 minutes
medium-boiled 6 minutes
hard-boiled 8 minutes

- Once cooked, use a slotted spoon to remove from the pan. Place in an egg cup and tap the top with the back of a teaspoon. Carefully slice off the top with a spoon. Serve with toast.

2

SCRAMBLED EGG

Scrambled eggs are delicious on their own or as part of a cooked breakfast. You can add different ingredients, such as bacon.

INGREDIENTS

This recipe is for 1 person. It takes 2 minutes to prepare and 8 minutes to cook.

- 1 slice of streaky bacon (optional)
- 1 tbsp milk
- 1 egg
- a small knob of butter
- dried basil, to serve
- 1 slice of toast, buttered

METHOD

- Ask an adult to grill the bacon. When it's cooked use a knife and fork to cut it up into small pieces.

- In a small glass bowl, use a hand whisk to mix together the milk and egg until creamy.

- Melt the butter in a small frying pan on medium heat, then add the egg and milk mixture. Stir often until the eggs are just cooked, but still creamy. Stir in the grilled bacon pieces with a wooden spoon, if using.

- Sprinkle the dried basil over the eggs and serve on toast.

SHAPES & SIZES

Most of the eggs we eat come from hens, but you can buy lots of different types. Go ahead and eggs-periment.

Quail Duck Hen Gull Goose Ostrich

3

MASALA OMELETTE

The spices and fresh herbs in this omelette will give a great kick-start to your day. If you like, you could add some chopped garlic in step 1.

INGREDIENTS

- 1 tbsp vegetable oil
- 1 tsp cumin seeds
- 1 medium onion, chopped
- 1 green chilli, deseeded and chopped
- ½ tsp turmeric powder
- 1 medium tomato, chopped
- 2 tbsp chopped coriander
- 4 eggs, beaten with a pinch of salt
- ¼ tsp ground pepper
- 2 tbsp finely grated cheese

METHOD

- Heat the oil in a non-stick frying pan. Add the cumin, onion, chilli, and turmeric. Sauté for about 2 minutes, until the onions are soft.

- Add the tomato and coriander, and sauté for a few more seconds.

- Add the beaten eggs and pepper, and gently swirl the pan to spread the eggs evenly. When the eggs begin to set, sprinkle over the grated cheese.

- When the cheese is just melted and eggs have set completely, flip over half the omelette to fold it. Remove onto a plate and serve hot with toast.

4

FRIED EGG

Fried eggs are quick to make and are a good way to have a filling breakfast. They are best served in a roll or on toast.

INGREDIENTS

This recipe is for 1 person. It takes 1 minute to prepare and 2-4 minutes to cook.

- 1 tsp sunflower oil
- 1 egg
- 1 bread roll, halved and buttered

METHOD

- Ask an adult to heat the oil in a pan over medium heat.

- Crack the egg into a bowl. If any of the shell falls into the bowl, scoop it out using a spoon. Gently tip the egg into the frying pan.

- The egg needs to be fried for about 2 minutes on medium heat. If you like your egg well-done, it needs to be cooked on both sides. Serve the fried egg on a buttered bread roll.

17

POHA WITH PEANUTS

For a quick, filling breakfast, fluffy, flavourful poha is an excellent choice. Don't leave out the lemon juice – it really perks up this dish!

INGREDIENTS

- 125g (4½oz) poha (thick variety)
- 2 tbsp vegetable oil
- ½ tsp mustard seeds
- ⅛ tsp asafetida
- 1 dried red chilli, broken
- ½ tsp turmeric powder
- 6-8 curry leaves
- 4 tbsp roasted peanuts
- salt
- juice of 1 lemon
- 2 tbsp finely chopped coriander (optional)

TOOLS

- strainer
- fork
- pan or wok
- wooden spatula
- bowl

1 Put the poha in a strainer placed over a bowl. Pour 120ml (4fl oz) water over – just enough to moisten it. Fluff with a fork and set aside.

2 Heat the oil in a pan over medium heat. Add the mustard seeds and stir until they pop.

3 Add the asafetida, chilli, turmeric, curry leaves, and peanuts. Cook, stirring for about 3 minutes or until the mixture becomes fragrant.

4 Add the poha and salt to the mixture, and gently mix until well combined.

5

Stir in the lemon juice and garnish with the chopped coriander, if using. Serve hot.

TOP TIP

You can add boiled potatoes and green vegetables of your choice at step 3 to make this dish more nutritious and filling.

CHILLA

A gram flour pancake, chilla is a great vegetarian breakfast. It tastes best when served warm, with tomato sauce or your favourite chutney.

Serves 6 | Prep 15 mins | Cook 30 mins

INGREDIENTS

- 140g (5oz) gram flour
- 1 medium onion, finely chopped
- 1 green chilli, deseeded and finely chopped
- 4 tbsp finely chopped coriander
- salt, to taste
- 3 tbsp vegetable oil

TOOLS

- mixing bowl
- whisk
- non-stick frying pan or skillet
- spatula

1

In a mixing bowl, combine the gram flour, onion, chilli, coriander, and salt and mix well. Gradually add 175ml (6fl oz) water and whisk to make a smooth batter. Whisk continuously to avoid any lumps in the batter.

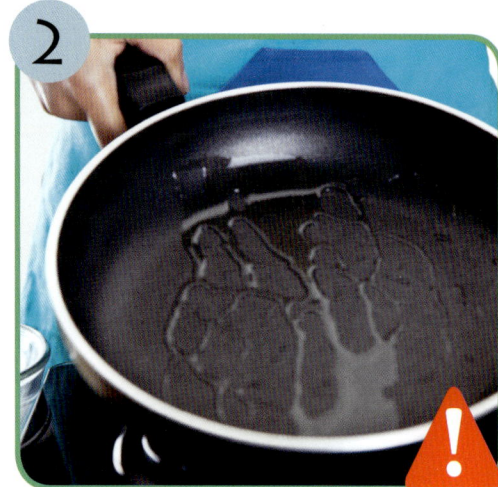

2

Heat 1 teaspoon of the oil in a non-stick frying pan, and swirl it so it coats the base evenly.

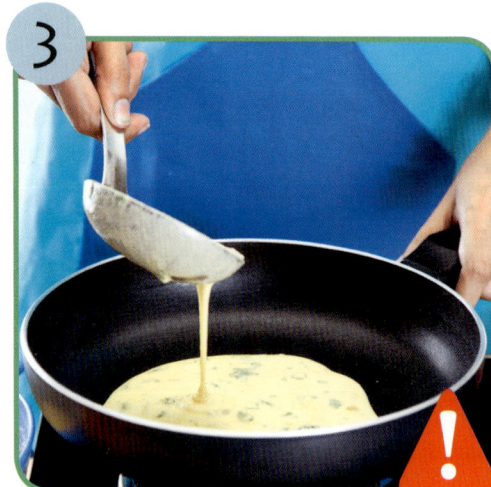

3

Pour 125ml (4fl oz) of the batter in the centre of the pan. Spread it around by gently swirling the pan. Cook until it begins to set and turns golden in colour.

4

Carefully flip the chilla and continue to cook on the other side until it is cooked through. Wipe the frying pan with a damp cloth and repeat the process.

FRUITY CEREALS

You need a hearty breakfast to keep you going through the morning. This recipe will keep you filled up until lunchtime.

Serves 8 | Prep 5 mins | Cook 20 mins

1

Ask an adult to preheat the oven to 200°C (400°F/Gas 6). Heat the oil and golden syrup or honey in a saucepan over low heat.

2

Pour the oil and golden syrup mixture into a large bowl with the oats, hazelnuts, and pumpkin seeds.

3

Tip the mixture onto a baking tray and spread it out. Bake in the oven for 10 minutes or until the cereal turns a golden-brown colour.

4

Let the mixture cool and then tip it into a bowl. Add the banana chips and raisins, and stir well. Serve with milk or plain yogurt.

INGREDIENTS

- 2 tbsp sunflower oil
- 6 tbsp golden syrup or runny honey
- 350g (12oz) rolled oats
- 115g (4oz) hazelnuts
- 60g (2oz) pumpkin seeds
- 115g (4oz) dried, unsalted banana chips, broken into small pieces
- 115g (4oz) raisins
- milk or plain yogurt, to serve

TOOLS

- saucepan
- spatula
- large bowls
- baking tray

TOP TIP

You can replace the hazelnuts with walnuts or unsalted, roasted peanuts. Add fresh fruit to the cereal before eating, if you prefer.

PANCAKES & CRÊPES

Pancakes can be thick or thin, depending on the ingredients you use to make them. Have fun trying out both types of pancake. Thin pancakes are often called "crêpes". Make this dish for your family.

1

Crack the egg into a bowl. Add the flour, bicarbonate of soda, and milk. Whisk the mixture until it's smooth.

2

Ask an adult to heat a tablespoon of the oil in a frying pan. Use a large spoon to carefully pour the pancake mixture into the pan.

3

Fry the pancake until it is golden-brown on the bottom and bubbling on the top. Flip the pancake over and fry it on the other side until golden-brown. Serve the pancakes with strawberries and yogurt.

4

To make the crêpes, pour a ladleful of the batter in a non-stick frying pan and swirl it around. Make sure the batter coats the pan evenly. Cook on medium heat. Repeat with the remaining batter.

INGREDIENTS

For the pancakes
- 1 egg
- 110g (3³/₄oz) self-raising flour
- 1 tsp bicarbonate of soda
- 150ml (5fl oz) milk
- sunflower oil, for frying
- 200g (7oz) fresh strawberries, hulled and sliced
- 4 tbsp plain yogurt

For the crêpes
- 110g (3³/₄oz) plain flour
- 1 large egg
- 280ml (9¹/₂fl oz) milk
- 1 sliced banana and chocolate sauce or lemon juice and sugar, to serve

TOOLS
- bowl
- whisk
- non-stick frying pan
- large spoon
- spatula

FRUIT BARS

Cereal bars are perfect for breakfast or as a healthy snack. Once you've mastered this recipe, experiment with other fruit and nuts.

INGREDIENTS

- 115g (4oz) unsalted butter, plus extra for greasing
- 100g (3½oz) light brown sugar
- 115g (4oz) golden syrup or runny honey
- 300g (10oz) rolled oats
- 100g (3½oz) raisins
- 50g (1¾oz) mixed nuts, chopped

TOOLS

- 30 x 23 x 4cm (12 x 9 x 1½in) baking tin
- baking parchment
- wooden spoon
- saucepan

STICKY STUFF

The sugar and golden syrup act like a glue in this recipe. They help the dry ingredients to stick together, making the muesli bars incredibly chewy and sticky!

1

Ask an adult to preheat the oven to 150°C (300°F/Gas 2). Grease the baking tin, then line it with 2 sheets of baking parchment.

2

Melt the butter, sugar, and golden syrup or runny honey in a saucepan over low heat.

3

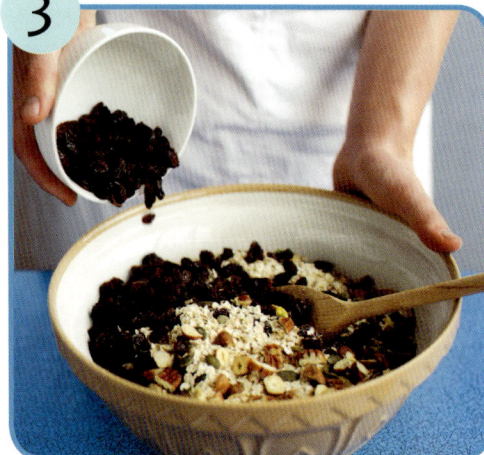

Place all the other ingredients in a large bowl and pour in the sugar mixture.

4

Spread the mixture evenly in the baking tin and, using a masher, press it down firmly so it sticks together. Bake for 20–30 minutes or until golden-brown.

5

When the cereal bars are baked, leave them to cool for 5 minutes. Then, using a cloth to hold the tin, cut them into 12 squares with a knife. Remove them from the tin when fully cooled and firm.

LUNCH BOX

CHICKEN PASTA SALAD

This mildly spiced pasta and chicken salad makes a perfect light lunch and is also ideal for a school sandwich box.

Serves 4 | 10 mins Prep | 15 mins Cook

1

Bring a large pan of lightly salted water to the boil. Add the pasta and cook according to pack instructions. Drain and rinse under cold running water.

2

Meanwhile, in a small frying pan, heat the oil, add the curry paste and spring onions, and cook for 2 minutes. Leave to cool.

3

Cut away the two sides of the mango, close to the stone. Cut the flesh into criss-cross patterns, press each half inside out, and carefully cut off the cubes.

4

Place the spice mixture in a bowl and stir in the lemon juice, yogurt, mayonnaise, and coriander. Add the chicken, mango, and grapes. Chill until ready to eat.

INGREDIENTS

- salt
- 125g (4oz) farfalle pasta
- 2 tsp sunflower oil
- 1 tbsp curry paste
- 3 spring onions, chopped
- 1 ripe mango
- juice of ½ lemon
- 100ml (3½fl oz) low fat yogurt
- 100ml (3½fl oz) mayonnaise
- 350g (12oz) cooked chicken breast, diced
- 2 tbsp chopped coriander
- 150g (5½oz) red and green grapes, halved

TOOLS

- large saucepan
- small frying pan
- wooden spoon
- knife
- mixing bowl

29

FOUR WAYS WITH PIZZAS

Try out these classic and new pizzas.

TINY TOMS PIZZA

This is a classic combination of ingredients and flavours. Restaurants that serve pizza would have this at the top of their list.

INGREDIENTS

- pizza dough (see page 13)
- flour, for dusting
- 2-3 tbsp tomato purée or passata
- 1 ball of mozzarella cheese
- 200g (7oz) cherry tomatoes
- fresh basil leaves, to serve

METHOD

- Roll out your pizza dough on a floured surface into a circle that will fit your pizza tray.
- Spread the tomato purée or passata over the pizza using the back of a spoon.
- Carefully cut the mozzarella ball into slices.
- Place the mozzarella slices onto the pizza (slightly overlapping) and scatter the tomatoes on the cheese.
- Bake the pizza in a preheated oven, 180°C (350°F/Gas 4) for 20 minutes.
- Garnish with a handful of torn, fresh basil leaves.

HAWAIIAN BITES

These are a fun take on ham and pineapple pizza. They'll be snapped up quickly, so make sure you try one before they all go!

INGREDIENTS

- flour, for dusting
- pizza dough (see page 13)
- 2-3 tbsp tomato purée or passata
- 212g can pineapple pieces, drained
- 60g (2oz) ham, cut into strips
- 150g (5½oz) grated mozzarella cheese

METHOD

- On a floured surface, divide your pizza dough into 12 small balls. Flatten the balls so they form small circles that are about 8cm (3in) in diameter.
- Spread the tomato purée or passata over the dough circles using the back of a spoon.
- Place a couple of pineapple pieces and a few strips of ham onto each pizza.
- Sprinkle a little bit of grated mozzarella cheese over each pizza bite.
- Bake the pizzas in a preheated oven, 180°C (350°F/Gas 4) for 15 minutes.

Pineapple

Anchovies

Baby spinach leaves

Sliced sweet peppers

Olives

Chilli peppers

Pepperoni

Cherry tomatoes

3

4

MUSHROOM MADNESS

If you're a pizza fan, then this option will be right up your street. The mushrooms and mozzarella will melt in your mouth.

INGREDIENTS

- 1 tbsp olive oil
- 125g (4½oz) mushrooms, sliced
- pizza dough (see page 13)
- flour, for dusting
- 2-3 tbsp tomato purée or passata
- 1 ball of mozzarella cheese

METHOD

- Gently heat the oil in a frying pan and fry the mushrooms for 2 minutes.
- Roll out your pizza dough on a floured surface into a circle that will fit your pizza tray. Roll the dough as thinly as you can.
- Spread the tomato sauce or passata over the pizza using the back of a spoon.
- Cut the mozzarella ball into thin slices.
- Place the mozzarella slices and mushrooms onto the pizza.
- Bake the pizza in a preheated oven, 180°C (350°F/ Gas 4) for 20 minutes.

PIZZA-POPS

These fun lollipop-style pizzas are great for a party or picnic. The combination of peppers and tomatoes is delicious.

INGREDIENTS

- pizza dough (see page 13)
- 12 small lollipop sticks
- 2-3 tbsp tomato purée or passata
- 150g (5½oz) grated mozzarella cheese
- ½ a yellow pepper, sliced
- 6 red cherry tomatoes, halved
- 6 yellow cherry tomatoes, halved

METHOD

- Divide your pizza dough into 12 small balls. Flatten the balls so they form small circles that are approximately 8cm (3in) in diameter. Insert a stick into each uncooked dough circle.
- Spread the tomato sauce over the circles using the back of a spoon.
- Decorate with grated mozzarella, peppers, and tomatoes.
- Bake the pizzas in a preheated oven, 180°C (350°F/Gas 4) for 15 minutes.

CRISPY ALOO TIKKIS

Semolina gives these tikkis, or potato cakes, a crisp, golden-brown crust. Perfect for an evening snack, these tikkis taste great with some green chutney or tomato ketchup.

Serves 4 | **Prep 20 mins** | **Cook 20 mins**

1

Boil the potatoes in salted water until tender. Once cool enough to handle, peel and cut in half. Mash the potatoes well using a fork or potato masher.

2

Add the flour, semolina, chillies, onion, cumin, cayenne, coriander, and salt to taste. Knead until smooth and divide into 12 pieces.

3

Take a portion and flatten it on your palm, shaping it into a 1cm (½in) thick cake.

4

Heat the oil in a frying pan and add the cakes carefully. Cook them gently in batches. Fry on both sides until golden brown. Remove and drain on kitchen paper. Make ahead and rewarm, or serve at room temperature.

INGREDIENTS

- 450g (1lb) potatoes
- salt
- 30g (1oz) all-purpose flour
- 175g (6oz) semolina
- 2 green chillies, deseeded and finely chopped
- 1 medium red onion, finely chopped
- 1 tsp toasted cumin powder
- 1 tsp cayenne pepper
- 45g (1½oz) fresh coriander, chopped
- 2 tbsp vegetable oil, for shallow frying

TOOLS

- boiling pan
- knife
- fork or potato masher
- frying pan
- slotted spoon
- kitchen paper

TOP TIP

Add peas and cheese to make the tikkis more delicious and nutritious. You can even make them with sweet potatoes or yams for a new twist.

FOUR WAYS WITH SAUCES & CHUTNEY

Try these simple and versatile dipping sauces and a chutney.

1

CHUNKY TOMATO SAUCE

This sauce is hearty and full of flavour – use in a lasagne or as a simple sauce for a pasta dish.

INGREDIENTS

- 1 onion
- 1 garlic clove
- 2 tbsp olive oil
- 400g can tomatoes
- 1 tbsp tomato purée

METHOD

- Chop the onion into small pieces and crush the garlic clove.

- Pour the oil into a saucepan and add the onion and garlic. Fry gently for 2 minutes or until the onion is golden.

- Add the tomatoes and purée to the saucepan, stir, and cook for 3 minutes.

2

CRUNCHY SATAY SAUCE

You can use smooth peanut butter for this sauce, but crunchy peanut butter gives it a better texture.

INGREDIENTS

- 1½ onions
- 3cm (1½in) piece fresh ginger
- 3 garlic cloves
- 4½ tbsp vegetable oil
- 3 tbsp soy sauce
- 4½ tbsp light brown sugar
- 225g (8oz) crunchy peanut butter
- juice of 2 limes

METHOD

- Peel the onions and chop very finely. Peel the ginger and grate it coarsely, then peel and crush the garlic.

- Heat the oil in a saucepan. Cook the onion for 3 minutes or until soft. Add the ginger and garlic and cook for a few minutes. Let the mixture cool.

- Place the onion mixture, soy sauce, sugar, peanut butter, and lime juice in a bowl with 128ml (4fl oz) of water, and whisk.

Saucepan

Wooden spoon

Whisk

Knife

3

4

CHEESY WHITE SAUCE

This sauce is often used in lasagne (see pages 76–77). You can also put it on pasta and add cooked bacon to make a cheesy, creamy pasta.

INGREDIENTS

- 60g (2oz) unsalted butter

- 30g (1oz) plain flour

- 500ml (16fl oz) warm milk

- 60g (2oz) Parmesan cheese, grated

METHOD

- In a small pan, melt the butter over low heat.

- Stir in the flour and cook for 1 minute. Gradually whisk in the milk. Stir and continue heating until thickened.

- Add in the cheese and season. Stir until the cheese is well mixed into the sauce.

TAMARIND & RAISIN CHUTNEY

This sweet and sour chutney is a delicious combination of tamarind and raisins. It is best enjoyed in a chaat or tossed with fresh fruits.

INGREDIENTS

- 120ml (4fl oz) tamarind paste

- 225g (8oz) sugar

- 1 tsp cumin, roasted and ground

- ½ tsp ground red chilli

- salt

- 100g (3½oz) raisins

METHOD

- Place all the ingredients with 120ml (4fl oz) water in a pan over high heat.

- Bring to the boil, then simmer gently for about 8–10 minutes until all the flavours are well combined and the chutney is thick.

- Leave to cool and then spoon into airtight jars. Store in a refrigerator for up to a month.

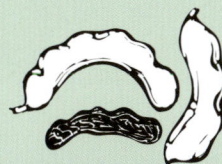

BASIC BREAD

This recipe is easy and fun to make. Use the dough for a traditional loaf or for delicious rolls instead (you can make eight rolls with this dough).

Makes 1 loaf   Prep 1 3/4 hours   Cook 30 mins

1

Lightly grease the loaf tin with butter, and set aside. Place the yeast, sugar, and a little of the water in a small bowl. Stir well and leave in a warm place for 10 minutes until frothy.

2

Sift the flour and salt into a large mixing bowl. Make a well in the centre and pour in the yeast mixture and the remaining water. Stir to form a dough. Knead the dough for 10 minutes on a floured surface.

3

Place the dough back in the bowl, cover with a damp kitchen towel and leave in a warm place for an hour. "Knock back" the dough, by lightly punching it. (This knocks out the large air bubbles.)

4

Ask an adult to preheat the oven to 220°C (425°F/Gas 7). Then, knead the dough lightly on a floured surface.

5

Shape the dough into a rectangle and tuck the ends under to fit into the tin. Place in the tin. Cover with the damp kitchen towel and leave to prove in a warm place for a further 30 minutes.

6

Place the tin in the centre of the oven. Bake for 30 minutes or until risen and golden. Turn out the loaf and tap the base – it should sound hollow. Place on a cooling rack.

INGREDIENTS

- butter for greasing
- 1½ tsp dried yeast
- 1 tsp caster sugar
- 360ml (12fl oz) lukewarm water
- 500g (1lb 2oz) strong white bread flour, plus extra for dusting
- 2 tsp salt

Tools

- 1lb loaf tin
- sieve
- mixing bowl
- cling film
- cooling rack

TOP TIP

To make bread rolls, divide the dough into 8 balls at step 5. Place on a greased baking sheet and flatten a bit. Cover with a damp tea towel and leave to rise for 30 minutes. Brush the tops with milk and bake for 20 minutes.

CLUB SANDWICH

This triple-decker deluxe lunch uses ham, chicken, and cheese. However, you can choose any ingredients you like to build your own stackable sandwich.

Serves 4

10 mins Prep

INGREDIENTS

- 6 slices of white bread
- 4 tbsp mayonnaise
- 1 tbsp lemon juice
- salt and freshly ground black pepper
- 50 (1¾oz) iceberg lettuce, shredded
- 2 slices ham
- 2 slices Swiss or Cheddar cheese
- 1 tomato, sliced
- 50g (1¾oz) cooked chicken breast, shredded

TOOLS

- bread knife
- cutting board
- mixing bowl
- metal spoon
- toothpicks

1 Lightly toast the bread on both sides in a toaster or under a preheated moderate grill. Cut off the crusts.

2 In a small bowl, mix together the mayonnaise and lemon juice. Season to taste and then stir in the shredded lettuce.

3 Spread 2 slices of the white toast with half of the lettuce and mayonnaise mixture.

4 Place a slice of ham, then a slice of cheese on top of each. Top with another slice of toast and spread with the remaining lettuce and mayonnaise mixture.

5 Add some slices of tomato and the chicken. Top with the remaining slice of toast.

6 Cut each sandwich into 4 triangles and secure each one with a toothpick.

39

PITTA POCKETS

Tofu is a versatile and nutritious ingredient. The sauce used in this recipe gives the tofu a yummy barbecue taste as well as an appealing glow.

INGREDIENTS

- 250g (9oz) firm tofu
- a little olive oil
- 4 wholemeal pitta bread, warmed in a toaster or oven
- 3 crisp lettuce leaves, shredded
- 2 spring onions, peeled and cut into long strips
- handful of alfalfa sprouts, (optional)

For the marinade
- 2 tbsp sweet chilli sauce
- 2 tbsp tomato ketchup
- 2 tbsp soy sauce
- 1/2 tsp ground cumin

TOOLS
- small sharp knife
- chopping board
- kitchen towel
- dessert spoon
- shallow dish
- griddle pan
- spatula and tongs

1

In a shallow dish, mix together all the ingredients for the marinade. Set aside. Pat the tofu dry with a kitchen towel and cut it into 8 long slices.

2

Place the tofu into the dish with the marinade. Spoon the marinade over the tofu until it is well coated. Leave to marinate for at least 1 hour.

3

Brush the griddle pan with the olive oil and then put it on high heat. Carefully put 4 of the tofu slices onto the hot pan.

4

Cook the tofu for 4 minutes on each side or until golden. As you cook, spoon over more of the marinade. Griddle the rest of the tofu in the same way.

TOP TIP
Strips of chicken, pork, turkey, or even a medley of vegetables such as pepper, courgette, and onion make a great alternative to the tofu.

5

Carefully slice along the edge of the pitta bread. Divide the lettuce, spring onions, and alfalfa sprouts between the pitta bread and then add 2 pieces of tofu.

RED PEPPER HUMMUS

This roasted red pepper hummus makes a perfect dip for snacking with toasted pitta or crudités. Alternatively, spread onto tortillas with some crumbled feta cheese for an easy wrap.

INGREDIENTS

- 2 red peppers, deseeded and cut into 4
- 400g (14oz) can chickpeas, drained and rinsed
- 2 garlic cloves, peeled
- 2 tbsp tahini (sesame seed paste)
- juice of ½ lemon
- 45ml (1.5fl oz) olive oil
- a little paprika

TOOLS

- knife
- food processor
- plastic bag
- bowl

1

Place the red peppers under a hot grill. Grill until the skins have blackened. Place in a plastic bag and when cool, peel off the blackened skin.

2

Place the skinless peppers with the remaining ingredients in a food processor and blend until smooth and creamy.

3

Transfer the hummus to a bowl and sprinkle with a little paprika. Serve with grilled pitta breads or vegetable crudités.

DID YOU KNOW?

Hummus is one of the world's oldest known prepared foods, with evidence suggesting use of chickpeas by ancient Egyptians 7,000 years ago.

FRESH TOMATO PASTA

You don't need to cook the sauce for this pasta dish. It's deliciously fresh and fast to make. The classic flavours of tomato and basil are perfect together.

Serves 4 | Prep 5 mins | Cook 10 mins

1

Put the tomatoes, garlic, basil, and olive oil in a large bowl and season with black pepper. Stir the mixture together using a wooden spoon.

2

Ask an adult to cook the pasta in a saucepan of salted boiling water. Using a colander, drain the pasta well, then toss with the tomato sauce. Sprinkle the cheese before serving.

INGREDIENTS

- 5 tomatoes, deseeded and roughly chopped
- 2 garlic cloves, finely chopped
- handful of basil leaves, torn
- 2 tbsp extra virgin olive oil
- freshly ground black pepper
- 200g (7oz) farfalle pasta
- salt
- freshly grated Parmesan cheese, to serve

TOOLS

- large glass bowl
- wooden spoon
- large saucepan
- colander

44

POTATO WEDGES

These wedges are a healthy and easy alternative to chips, but just as delicious. You can make them spicy by adding paprika or fajita seasoning.

Serves 4 | Prep 15 mins | Cook 30 mins

1

Ask an adult to preheat the oven to 200°C (400°F/Gas 6). Cut each potato lengthways into thick wedges.

2

Put the oil, salt, and pepper into a bowl. Add the paprika or fajita seasoning, if using. Then, add the potatoes and mix thoroughly.

3

Lay the wedges on a baking tray lined with parchment. Bake the wedges for 30 minutes, turning 2–3 times during cooking. They'll be lovely and golden when they're cooked.

INGREDIENTS

- 2 large potatoes
- 1 tbsp olive oil
- salt and freshly ground pepper
- ½ tsp paprika or fajita seasoning (optional)

TOOLS

- small sharp knife
- chopping board
- kitchen towel
- scissors
- baking tray
- baking parchment
- spatula and tongs

Cheese & Pesto Straws

Flavoured with pesto and cheese, these light crisp straws are perfect for dipping.

Makes 30 | Prep 25 mins | Cook 15 mins

1

Ask an adult to preheat the oven to 180°C (350°F/Gas 4). Sift the flour into a bowl with a pinch of salt. Add the butter and rub in until it looks like fine breadcrumbs.

2

Stir in 75g (3oz) of the cheeses. Beat together the egg and egg yolk and stir into the flour with the pesto sauce. Mix to a dough.

3

The mixture should be of the consistency where you can roll it into a ball.

4

On a lightly floured surface, roll out the dough into a rectangle about 28 x 23cm (11 x 9in). Cut in half down the longest length, then cut each into about 15 straws.

5

Line a baking tray with baking parchment. Transfer the straws to the baking sheet, leaving some space between each.

6

Sprinkle over the remaining cheese and chill for 15 minutes. Bake for 12–15 minutes. Cool for 5 minutes on the tray, then transfer to a cooling rack.

INGREDIENTS

- 200g (7oz) plain flour
- 125g (4½oz) chilled butter, cut into small cubes
- 50g (2oz) Gruyère or Cheddar cheese, finely grated
- 50g (2oz) Parmesan cheese, finely grated
- 1 whole egg, plus 1 yolk
- 2 tbsp pesto sauce (either red or green)
- 50g (1¾oz) cooked chicken breast, shredded

TOOLS

- sieve
- rolling pin
- mixing bowl
- metal spoon
- knife
- baking parchment
- baking tray
- cooling rack

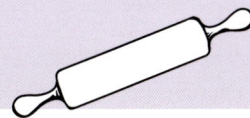

TOP TIP

While sprinkling the cheese before baking, you can also sprinkle some sesame seeds for a nice flavour and crunch.

CORNBREAD

This cornbread recipe is really simple to make, and the sweetcorn and spring onions give it an unusual texture.

INGREDIENTS

- oil or butter, for greasing
- 125g (4½oz) plain flour
- 125g (4½oz) cornmeal or polenta
- 1 tbsp baking powder
- 1 tsp salt
- 5 spring onions, finely chopped, (optional)
- 150g (5½oz) can sweetcorn
- 2 eggs
- 284ml carton buttermilk or natural yogurt
- 100ml (3½fl oz) milk
- 50g (1¾oz) butter, melted and cooled

TOOLS

- 20cm (8in) square cake tin or a 20cm (8in) pie dish, ceramic or metal
- pastry brush
- large mixing bowl
- wooden spoon
- measuring jug
- whisk
- oven gloves
- sharp knife

1

Grease a 20cm (8in) square cake tin or a round 20cm (8in) ceramic pie dish. Preheat the oven to 200°C (400°F/Gas 6).

2

In a large mixing bowl, place the flour, cornmeal or polenta, baking powder, salt, spring onions, and sweetcorn. Mix together thoroughly with a wooden spoon and set aside.

3

In a measuring jug, whisk together the eggs, buttermilk or yogurt, milk, and melted butter with a hand whisk until they are thoroughly combined and frothy.

4

Pour the egg and milk mixture into the flour mixture in the mixing bowl. Stir with a wooden spoon to combine all the ingredients thoroughly.

5

Pour the mixture into the prepared tin. Bake for 25–30 minutes until golden-brown, and beginning to pull away from the sides of the tin. Allow to cool in the tin before cutting into wedges.

RICE BALLS

This dish works well as a light main meal or as a filling starter. The soft rice and melted mozzarella are tasty and have a great texture.

TOP TIP

Add variety to this light meal by serving it with a mixture of steamed vegetables or a fresh garden salad with leaves, cherry tomatoes, and cucumber slices.

1

Generously season the rice with black pepper and stir with a spoon to make sure the pepper is well mixed. Roll the rice into 12 evenly sized balls.

2

Make a hole in each rice ball. Push a cube of mozzarella cheese into the centre of each ball, then cover so that the cheese is enclosed.

3

Roll each ball in the egg and then roll in the breadcrumbs (bread or toast that's been turned into crumbs in a food processor – see page 9 for how to make breadcrumbs).

4

Deep-fry the balls in the oil over medium heat for 2–3 minutes or until golden. Place the balls on kitchen paper to soak some oil. Serve the balls with salad and salsa.

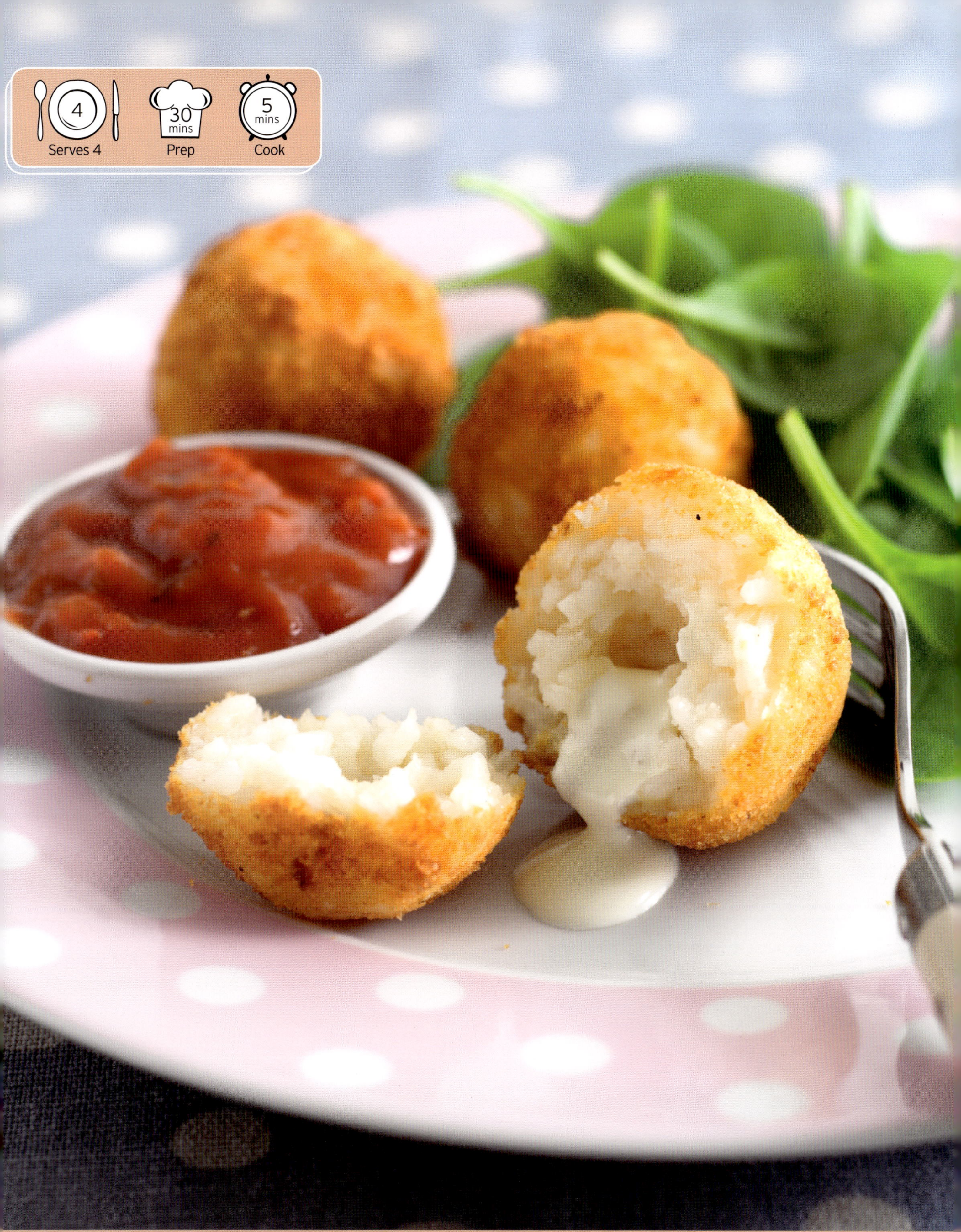
4
Serves 4
30 mins
Prep
5 mins
Cook

FOUR WAYS WITH STARTERS

Try out these tasty bruschettas.

1

2

TINY TOMATOES

This is a delicious combination of ingredients and flavours. The mozzarella melts in your mouth, and the tomatoes are so juicy.

INGREDIENTS

• This recipe is for 4 people. It takes 5 minutes to prepare and 2 minutes to cook.

• ciabatta loaf, sliced

• 125g (4¹/₂oz) mini mozzarella balls

• 200g (7¹/₄oz) of cherry tomatoes

• 8 basil leaves

METHOD

• Toast the slices of ciabatta until golden under a grill. You may have 1 or 2 slices left over at the end.

• Carefully slice the cherry tomatoes in half.

• Place the mozzarella balls and tiny tomatoes on the toasted slices of ciabatta.

• Scatter a couple of basil leaves on each slice of ciabatta.

• Serve as individual portions or on a large tray.

CRISS-CROSS HAM

The salty ham and melted cheese make this bruschetta a yummy starter. It will be a real winner with your friends and family.

INGREDIENTS

• This recipe is for 4 people. It takes 5 minutes to prepare and 4 minutes to cook.

• ciabatta loaf, sliced

• 125g (4¹/₂oz) ham

• 170g (6oz) Cheddar cheese

METHOD

• Toast the slices of ciabatta until golden under a grill. You may have 1 or 2 slices left over at the end.

• Cut the ham into thin strips and the cheese into generous slices.

• Place the cheese slices onto the ciabatta, and then add the ham in a criss-cross pattern.

• Grill the bruschettas for 2 minutes or until the cheese begins to bubble. Be careful not to let the ham get overcooked.

• Serve as individual portions or on a large tray.

Cheese

Baby spinach leaves

Red pepper

Roasted vegetables

Tomatoes

Salami

Basil

3

CARROT BUTTER

The moist carrots and rich butter make this bruschetta a real favourite. You can keep any leftover mixture in the fridge for a few days.

INGREDIENTS

- This recipe is for 4 people. It takes 1 hour to prepare and 2 minutes to cook.
- 1 onion, finely chopped
- 1 tsp olive oil
- 4 carrots, finely grated
- 1 tsp tomato purée
- 1 tsp dried oregano
- 225g (8oz) butter
- ciabatta loaf, sliced
- coriander leaves to garnish (optional)

METHOD

- Fry the onions in the oil on medium heat.
- Blend the onion, carrots, tomato purée, oregano and butter in a food processor.
- Place the mixture in a bowl, cover, and refrigerate for 1 hour.
- Toast the slices of ciabatta under a grill until golden. You may have 1 or 2 slices left over.
- Generously spread the carrot butter onto the slices of toasted ciabatta and serve as individual portions or on a large platter.
- Garnish with coriander leaves, if desired.

4

CHEESE & CUCUMBER

These bright and fun bruschettas are great for a party. Use the remaining cucumber to make sticks to accompany the dish.

INGREDIENTS

- This recipe is for 4 people. It takes 5 minutes to prepare and 4 minutes to cook.
- ciabatta loaf, sliced
- 200g (7oz) cream cheese
- 1 cucumber

METHOD

- Toast the slices of ciabatta until golden under a grill. You may have 1 or 2 slices left over at the end.
- Spread the cheese evenly over the bread.
- Use a peeler carefully to peel a cucumber and use cookie cutters to make decorative shapes out of the peel and flesh of the cucumber.
- Place the shapes on the bruschettas and serve on individual plates or on a large platter.

VEGGIE SPRING ROLLS

These crispy spring rolls filled with vegetables make an easy and delicious snack. Serve with sweet chilli dipping sauce or soy sauce if you prefer.

Makes 12 | **Prep 15 mins** | **Cook 15 mins**

INGREDIENTS

- 100g (3½oz) beansprouts
- 50g (2oz) cabbage, shredded
- 1 carrot, cut into thin strips
- ½ red pepper, deseeded and thinly sliced
- 6 spring onions, thinly sliced
- 1 clove garlic, crushed
- 2.5cm (1in) piece root ginger, peeled and grated
- 1 tbsp dark soy sauce
- 6 sheets filo pastry
- 25g (1oz) melted butter

TOOLS

- mixing bowl
- wooden spoon
- cutting board
- knife
- small bowl
- pastry brush
- baking tray

1

Preheat the oven to 190°C (375°F/Gas 5). In a large bowl, mix together all the ingredients, except the filo pastry and butter.

2

Place the sheets of pastry on top of each other and cut in half.

3

Place 1 sheet of the pastry on a board and brush the edges with a little of the melted butter. Place some of the filling on the bottom edge.

4

Roll up, folding the ends over. Repeat with remaining pastry and filling.

5

Place on a baking tray and brush with butter. Bake for 12–15 minutes until golden. Serve with sweet chilli dipping sauce.

TOP TIP

You can use leftover dry vegetables as filling or even use sweetcorn, peas, or mushrooms, if you prefer.

POTATO SALAD

This simple potato salad is a classic. It substitutes traditional mayonnaise for a lighter creamy sauce, flavoured with fresh chives.

Serves 4 | Prep 5 mins | Cook 15 mins

1 Clean the potatoes thoroughly. Make sure there's no mud left on them. Cut any larger potatoes in half.

2 Cook in a pan of lightly salted boiling water for 12–15 minutes. Drain and allow to cool. Place in a mixing bowl.

3 In a small bowl, mix together the crème fraîche, yogurt, and chives.

4 Gently stir the chive mixture into the potatoes. Season to taste. Keep in the fridge until ready to serve.

FOUR WAYS WITH CHAAT

Experiment with different kinds of chaat.

1

2

ALOO CHAAT

If you like potatoes, you'll love this chaat. The mango powder adds a lovely sweet-sour flavour.

INGREDIENTS

- 900g (2lb) potatoes, boiled and peeled
- vegetable oil, for frying
- 1 large onion, finely chopped
- 2 green chillies, chopped
- 1 tsp mango powder
- 1 tsp garam masala
- 1 tsp roasted ground cumin
- salt, to taste
- juice of 2 lemons
- 1 tbsp chopped coriander

METHOD

- Cut the potatoes into 2.5cm (1in) rounds. Heat the oil to 180°C (350°F/Gas 4).
- Gently fry the potatoes until light golden-brown and very crisp.
- Using a slotted spoon, transfer them onto a kitchen towel to drain the excess oil.
- Arrange on a serving platter and evenly spread over all the other ingredients. Serve hot.

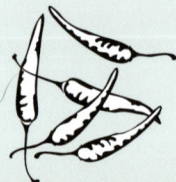

FRUIT CHAAT

This colourful fresh fruit chaat is both healthy and tasty. Feel free to experiment with your favourite fruits and choose the ones in season.

INGREDIENTS

- 1 red apple
- 1 ripe pear
- 1 guava
- 10-12 seedless grapes
- 1 banana
- 2 tbsp lemon juice
- 1 tbsp honey
- 1 tsp chaat masala
- ½ tsp ground red chilli
- 2 tbsp chopped mint leaves
- salt

METHOD

- Core and cut the apple, pear, and guava into 2.5cm (1in) pieces.
- Separate the grapes, cutting each into half, and slice the banana.
- Place the fruits in a bowl with all the remaining ingredients. Toss together gently and serve cold.

Pineapple

Lemon

Sliced sweet peppers

Tomatoes

Green mango

Cherry tomatoes

3

4

BHEL PURI

The tamarind chutney in this version of bhel puri makes it tangy, and the peanuts add a lovely crunch.

INGREDIENTS

- 50g (1³/₄oz) puffed rice
- 1 medium onion, chopped
- 1 medium potato, boiled, and cut into small cubes
- 60-85g (2-3oz) tamarind chutney (see p34-35)
- 60-85g (2-3oz) mint chutney
- 1 tbsp chaat masala
- salt, to taste
- 75g (2¹/₂oz) peanuts, roasted
- 4 tbsp finely chopped coriander

METHOD

- Combine all the ingredients in a large mixing bowl.
- Toss gently until all the ingredients are well mixed. Serve fresh.

SEV PURI

The chickpeas in this crunchy sev-topped chaat make it quite filling. Top with fresh coriander, instead of mint, if you prefer.

INGREDIENTS

- 12 shop-bought puris
- 2 boiled potatoes, peeled and finely chopped
- 125g (4¹/₂oz) boiled, drained chickpeas
- 1 onion, finely chopped
- 45g (1¹/₂oz) sev, or gram flour noodles
- 3 tbsp date-tamarind chutney
- 1 tbsp chopped mint

METHOD

- Arrange the puris on a plate.
- Top the puris with the potatoes, chickpeas, and onion, followed by the sev.
- Add the chutney to taste and garnish with the mint.

NACHOS & SALSA

Make this quick tomato salsa and spoon over tortilla chips with cheese for a tasty snack. You can even add some cooked diced chicken or kidney beans to make this snack more filling.

4 Serves 4 · **5 mins** Prep · **4 mins** Cook

1

Cut the tomatoes in half and remove the seeds, then dice. Place in a bowl and stir in all the remaining salsa ingredients.

2

Place the nachos on a large baking tray or shallow ovenproof dish and spoon over the salsa.

3

Scatter over the cheese. Place under a preheated grill for 3–4 minutes until the cheese has melted.

TOP TIP

Serve with sour cream and guacamole to dip your delicious nachos into.

INGREDIENTS

- 1 x 200g (7oz) pack plain tortilla chips
- 50g (2oz) mozzarella cheese, grated
- 50g (2oz) mature Cheddar cheese, grated

Salsa

- 350g (12oz) tomatoes
- ½ red onion, finely chopped
- 2 garlic cloves, crushed
- juice of ½ lime
- 4 tbsp chopped coriander
- ½ tsp sugar
- 1 green chilli, deseeded and chopped

TOOLS

- chopping board
- knife
- mixing bowl
- metal spoon
- baking tray

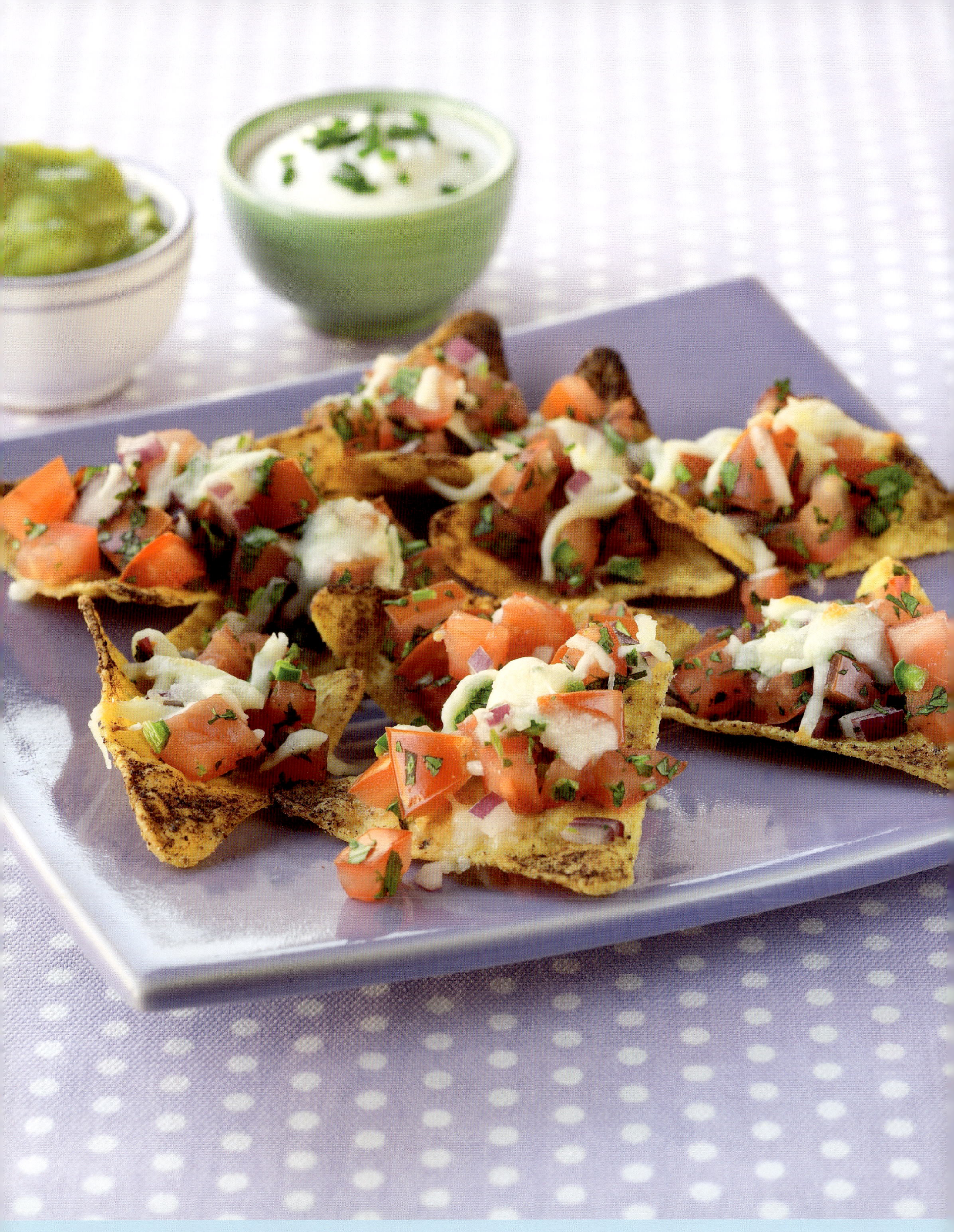

TOFFEE POPCORN

Home-made popcorn is great fun to make and tastes much better than shop-bought. If you prefer salted popcorn, just leave out the toffee sauce and sprinkle over some salt.

INGREDIENTS

- 2 tbsp corn oil
- 100g (3½oz) popping corn
- 50g (1¾oz) butter
- 50g (1¾oz) soft brown sugar
- 75ml (2½fl oz) golden syrup

TOOLS

- 2 medium saucepans
- large mixing bowl
- spoon

TOP TIP

Wait for 3-5 seconds between each "pop" before you turn off the heat.

1 Heat the oil in a saucepan. Add the corn and, with the lid on, shake to coat in the oil. Over medium heat, shake the pan occasionally until the corn has popped. Remove from the heat.

2 To make the toffee sauce, place the butter, sugar, and syrup in another pan. Stir together over medium heat until the butter has melted and the sugar has dissolved.

3 Put the popcorn into a large mixing bowl and drizzle the toffee sauce over the top.

4 Stir until the popcorn is coated. Stop stirring when the sauce has cooled and is setting. Leave until cool enough to eat.

SWEETCORN FRITTERS

These are popular in southern American states and are enjoyed best with friends and family. For big parties, simply double the quantities!

8-10 Makes 8-10 | 30 mins Prep | 15 mins Cook

1

Sieve the flour, baking powder, and salt into a large bowl.

2

Separate the egg by tipping the yolk from one half of the shell to the other. Let the egg white fall into one bowl. Drop the yolk into another.

3

Add the maple syrup and milk to the egg yolk and whisk together. Pour this mixture over the flour. Stir everything together to make a batter.

4

Then, whisk the egg white until it forms stiff peaks. Be careful not to overwhisk or it will go flat.

5

Use a spatula to fold the egg white into the flour mixture – carefully stirring around the side of the bowl and across the middle.

6

Tip the sweetcorn and spring onions into the batter mixture. Fold them in – be as light as you can here.

7

⚠️

Heat the oil, drop in tablespoons of the batter and cook for 1–2 minutes until the undersides are golden. Flip over, cook the other sides, then serve.

INGREDIENTS

- 30g (1oz) flour
- 1 tsp baking powder
- pinch of salt
- 1 egg
- 1 tbsp maple syrup
- 2 tbsp milk
- 200g (7oz) sweetcorn

- 2 spring onions, chopped
- 1-2 tbsp sunflower oil
- tomatoes and basil, to serve

TOOLS

- small bowl
- frying pan

- mixing bowl
- spatula
- whisk

MAIN MEALS

TOMATO & COUSCOUS SALAD

Salad makes a great light lunch or it can be eaten as an appetizer. This super salad is full of interesting ingredients and looks pretty on the plate. It's tasty, too!

1

Slice the tops off the tomatoes and scoop out the insides. Put the seeds and flesh into a bowl with the tomato juice.

2

Pour the boiling water over the couscous, cover, and leave to stand for 10 minutes. Then, use a fork to fluff up the grains.

3

Add the tomato mixture and stir. Add the sultanas, basil, and parsley (if using), and mix. Taste and season with the black pepper as needed.

4

Spoon the mixture into the reserved tomato shells. Finally, serve with any leftover couscous mixture and garnish with some lettuce leaves.

INGREDIENTS

- 4 large, firm tomatoes
- 150ml (5fl oz) tomato juice
- 125g (4½ oz) couscous
- 150ml (5fl oz) boiling water
- 50g (1¾ oz) sultanas
- handful of basil leaves, chopped
- handful of flat-leaf parsley, torn (optional)
- freshly ground black pepper
- lettuce leaves, to garnish

TOOLS

- sharp knife
- chopping board
- teaspoon
- small glass bowl
- large glass bowl
- fork
- tablespoon

TUNA & BEAN SALAD

Salads are good for you as they help you to get your five portions of fruit and vegetables a day. This salad is full of interesting ingredients and is fun to make.

INGREDIENTS

- 125g (4½oz) frozen broad beans
- 400g can tuna in olive oil, drained
- 10 cherry tomatoes, halved
- handful of fresh chives, finely chopped
- freshly ground black pepper
- 12 black olives, pitted
- 1 crisp lettuce such as Cos, leaves separated
- 2-3 spring onions, finely sliced

For the dressing
- 6 tbsp extra virgin olive oil
- 1 garlic clove, finely chopped
- 2 tbsp lemon juice
- 1-2 tsp Dijon mustard

TOOLS

- large glass bowl
- colander
- screw-top jar
- 4 serving bowls

1

Soak the broad beans in hot water for five minutes, then use a colander to drain. Set aside.

2

To make the dressing, put all the ingredients in a screw-top jar, season with black pepper, cover with the lid, and shake!

3

Put the tuna, tomatoes, and half of the dressing in a bowl. Sprinkle in half of the chives and season with the pepper. Gently mix in the beans and olives.

4

Spoon the tuna mixture on top of the lettuce. Drizzle with the remaining dressing, and sprinkle over the spring onions and remaining chives.

TOMATO SOUP

Soup is a comforting meal or snack and makes an easy starter to a main meal. This soup is wonderfully thick and creamy and is topped with small pieces of toast called croutons.

Serves 4

Prep 20 mins

Cook 35 mins

INGREDIENTS

- 1 small onion
- 1 small carrot
- 4 tbsp olive oil
- 1 garlic clove, crushed
- 1 tbsp plain flour
- 400g (14oz) can chopped tomatoes
- 1 tbsp tomato purée
- 1 tsp thyme leaves (optional)
- 450ml (15fl oz) vegetable stock
- a pinch of sugar
- a squeeze of lemon juice
- 2 thick slices of bread
- salt and freshly ground black pepper

TOOLS

- sharp knife
- peeler
- chopping board
- medium saucepan
- wooden spatula
- bread knife
- non-stick baking tray
- oven gloves
- ladle
- blender

1

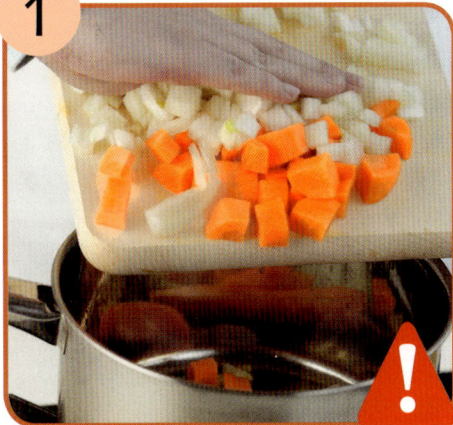

Peel and chop the onion and carrot. Ask an adult to preheat the oven to 220°C (425°F/Gas 7). Heat half the oil in a saucepan, over medium heat.

2

Add the onion and carrot and cook for about 5 minutes to soften, stirring occasionally. Stir in the garlic and flour and cook the mixture for 1 minute.

3

Add the tomatoes, purée, thyme, stock, sugar, and lemon juice to the pan and bring to the boil. Reduce the heat and simmer for 20–25 minutes.

4

While the soup is cooking, use cookie cutters to cut out shapes for the croutons. Scatter the bread on the baking tray, and drizzle over the remaining oil.

5

Use your hands to coat the bread in the oil and season. Bake for 8–10 minutes until crisp and golden. Flip after about 4 minutes for even cooking.

6

Carefully ladle the hot soup into the blender. Taste the soup, season with salt and pepper, if necessary, and blend until smooth. Ladle into bowls and serve with the croutons on top.

VEG NOODLES

A very quick dish to put together, vegetable noodles is delicious served hot, with a large dollop of tomato sauce.

4 Serves 4 | 20 mins Prep | 15 mins Cook

1

Bring a pot of water to the boil and add the noodles. Cook for 5–7 minutes, just enough to retain a slightly firm texture. Drain and set aside.

2

Heat the oil in a large skillet or wok over a medium heat. Add the ginger and garlic, and cook for 1 minute.

3

Add the soy sauce, chilli sauce, salt and pepper, and stir well to combine. Then, add the spring onion, green pepper, onion, and cabbage, and sauté for 2–3 minutes.

4

Add the noodles and mix to coat them with the vegetable mixture. Serve hot.

INGREDIENTS

- 225g (8oz) dried egg noodles or any noodles of your choice
- 2 tbsp vegetable oil
- 2.5cm (1in) fresh ginger, peeled and finely chopped
- 1 garlic clove, finely chopped
- 2 tbsp soy sauce
- ½ tbsp chilli sauce
- salt and freshly ground black pepper
- 1 spring onion, chopped
- 1 green pepper, thinly sliced
- 1 red onion, thinly sliced
- 35g (1oz) finely shredded cabbage

TOOLS

- pan with handles
- spaghetti spoon
- skillet or non-stick pan
- small bowls
- wooden spatula
- chopping board
- knife

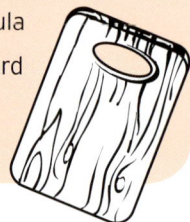

TOP TIP

Use any kind of noodles or add extra vegetables or tofu to make your own version. You can even add cooked, shredded chicken, if you prefer.

CHILLI PANEER

An Indian-Chinese classic, this dish goes wonderfully well with veg noodles (see pages 72–73). The soy sauce and spring onions add an authentic Oriental touch to it.

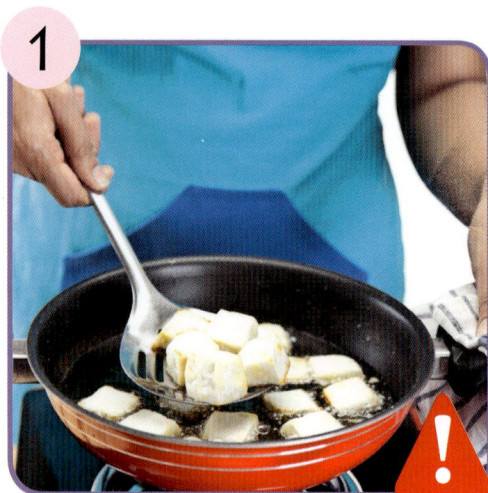

1

Heat the oil to 180°C (350°F/Gas 4). Carefully deep fry the paneer in batches until golden-brown. Remove with a slotted spoon and drain the excess oil on a kitchen paper.

2

Heat 2 tablespoons of oil in a wok over medium-high heat. Add the spring onions, ginger, and garlic, and cook for 2 minutes or until the mixture is fragrant.

3

Add the soy sauce, chilli flakes, cornstarch mixture, tomato sauce, and 2 tablespoons of water. Cook until the mixture is thick and smooth.

4

Stir in the green pepper, onion, and paneer, mixing until evenly coated. Season with salt, if required. Garnish with fresh coriander and serve hot.

INGREDIENTS

- 2 tbsp oil, plus extra for deep-frying
- 300g (10oz) fresh paneer, cut into cubes
- 2 spring onions, coarsely chopped
- 2.5cm (1in) fresh root ginger, peeled and finely chopped
- 3 garlic cloves, finely chopped
- 1 tbsp soy sauce
- 1 tsp chilli flakes, or more to taste
- 2 tbsp cornstarch combined with 1 tbsp water
- 1/2 tbsp tomato sauce
- 1 medium green pepper, cut into 2.5cm (1in) cubes
- 1 onion, cut into 2.5cm (1in) cubes
- salt (optional)
- 3 tbsp finely chopped coriander

TOOLS

- chopping board
- knife
- wok
- non stick pan
- slotted spoon
- wooden spatula

TOP TIP

You can substitute paneer with your favourite vegetables or tofu to make your own version of the dish. Addition of a fruit, such as pineapple, apple, peach, or orange adds a wonderful fragrance and sweetness to this dish.

VEGETABLE LASAGNE

A crowd-pleasing dish that's a meal in its own right, this lasagne makes a welcome change from the meat-based one. Why not experiment with other flavours?

Serves 6	Prep 50 mins	Cook 75 mins

1

Ask an adult to preheat the oven to 220°C (425°F/Gas 7). Cut the onions into wedges and then chop all the other vegetables into chunks.

2

In a roasting tin, mix the oil, rosemary, and garlic with the vegetables and season. Roast for 35 minutes, shaking the tin occasionally.

3

Gently warm through the tomatoes and tomato purée in a large saucepan. Take the pan off the heat and carefully stir in the roasted vegetables.

4

On low heat, melt the butter in a pan. Stir in the flour. Cook for 1 minute. Whisk in the milk. Stir until thickened. Add half the cheese and season.

5

Turn down the oven to 190°C (375°F/Gas 5). Spoon a third of the vegetables into the lasagne dish and top with 3 lasagne sheets.

6

Add another third of the vegetables, top with another layer of lasagne, pour over half the sauce, and then the remaining vegetables.

INGREDIENTS

- 2 large red onions
- 2 large carrots
- 2 large courgettes
- 2 red peppers, deseeded
- 1 medium aubergine
- 2 yellow peppers, deseeded
- 4 tbsp olive oil
- 2 tsp chopped fresh rosemary
- 2 garlic cloves, crushed
- salt and freshly ground black pepper
- 400g can chopped tomatoes
- 1 tbsp tomato purée
- 9 dried lasagne sheets

For the marinade
- 60g (2oz) unsalted butter
- 30g (1oz) plain flour
- 500ml (16fl oz) warm milk
- 125g (4½oz) Parmesan cheese, grated

TOOLS

- chopping board
- sharp knife
- roasting tin
- oven gloves
- large saucepan
- wooden spoon
- small saucepan
- whisk
- lasagne dish, preferably glass or ceramic, approx. 25 x 18cm and 5cm deep (10 x 7in and 2in deep)
- serving spoon

7

Lay on the remaining lasagne sheets and drizzle over the sauce. Sprinkle the cheese over the top and bake for 35 minutes or until golden and bubbling.

GRIDDLED CHICKEN

Food has a wonderful texture and finish to it when it's been cooked in a griddle pan. Always make sure you cook the meat thoroughly. You can eat this dish hot or cold.

Serves 4

Prep 45 mins

Cook 25 mins

INGREDIENTS

- 2 tsp paprika
- 5 tbsp olive oil
- 4 skinless chicken breasts, each about 150g (5½oz)
- 400g (14oz) baby new potatoes, cut in half, if necessary
- 8 cherry tomatoes
- 2 spring onions, finely chopped
- 3 tbsp chopped mint
- 1 tbsp lemon juice

TOOLS

- large shallow dish
- tablespoon
- cling film
- griddle pan
- tongs
- small sharp knife
- chopping board
- medium saucepan
- colander
- large glass bowl

1

Mix the paprika and 3 tablespoons of the oil in a large dish to make a marinade. Add the chicken and cover with cling film and chill for 30 minutes.

2

Heat a griddle pan until it is very hot. Reduce the heat to medium and place 2 chicken breasts in the pan. Griddle for 6 minutes on one side.

3

Carefully turn the chicken over using tongs. Spoon over a little of the marinade and then cook for 6 minutes or until cooked through. Griddle the remaining chicken.

4

Put the potatoes in a saucepan and cover with water. Bring to the boil and cook for 10 minutes or until they are tender.

5

Drain the potatoes and leave them to cool in a bowl. Halve the tomatoes. Place in the bowl with potatoes, then add the onions and mint.

6

Mix the remaining olive oil and lemon juice together using a fork. Then pour the mixture over the salad and stir well.

FOUR WAYS WITH RICE

These rice dishes are tasty and easy to make.

1

2

STEAMED RICE

Once you learn this basic recipe, you will be able to experiment with several other rice-based dishes.

INGREDIENTS

- 200g (7oz) long-grain basmati rice
- a pinch of salt

METHOD

- Place the rice in a strainer and rinse under cold water until the water runs clear.
- Place the rice and 120ml (4fl oz) water in a saucepan with a lid and bring to the boil over high heat. Add salt, cover, and reduce the heat to low.
- Simmer until the rice is tender (about 15 minutes). Remove from heat and let it sit covered for about 5 minutes.
- Fluff with a fork and serve hot.

CURD RICE

A south Indian favourite, this simple dish is best enjoyed with your favourite *achaar,* or pickle.

INGREDIENTS

- 350g (12oz) cooked rice
- 500g (1lb 2oz) plain yogurt
- 1 tbsp vegetable oil
- 1 tsp mustard seeds
- 2 tbsp split black lentils
- 1 green chilli, slit
- 10–12 curry leaves
- salt

METHOD

- Combine the rice and yogurt together in a bowl and keep aside.
- Heat the oil in a frying pan over medium heat. Add the mustard seeds and cook until they crackle.
- Add the lentils, green chilli, and curry leaves, stirring continuously for 2–3 minutes until fragrant.
- Using a tong, carefully remove half the curry leaves, and reserve.
- Add the rice-yogurt mixture and salt to the skillet. Mix well and cook for another minute. Serve hot, garnished with the reserved curry leaves.

Curry leaves

Spring onions

Mint

Onions

Coriander leaves

Tomatoes

3

LEMON RICE

Turmeric gives the rice its vibrant yellow colour. You could leave out either the red or green chillies.

INGREDIENTS

- 200g (7oz) basmati rice, rinsed and drained
- 1 tsp turmeric
- salt
- 2 tbsp vegetable oil
- 2 tsp mustard seeds
- 2 green chillies, deseeded and minced
- 5 tbsp raw cashew nuts
- 2 dried red chillies, crushed
- ¼ tsp asafetida
- 6 fresh curry leaves
- juice of 1 lemon

METHOD

- Boil the rice in 1 litre (1¾ pints) water with the turmeric and salt for about 10 minutes. Drain and cover to keep warm.

- Heat the oil in a heavy pan or skillet over medium heat. Add the mustard seeds and cook until they crackle.

- Add the green chillies, cashew nuts, red chillies, asafetida, and curry leaves, stirring continuously for 2–3 minutes until very fragrant.

- Stir in the rice and evenly mix all the ingredients.

- Remove from heat and stir in the lemon juice. Serve hot.

4

VEGETABLE PULAO

Choose all your favourite vegetables to use in this recipe. Try the pulao with your favourite raita.

INGREDIENTS

- 2 tbsp vegetable oil
- 1 bay leaf
- 5cm (2in) cinnamon stick
- 2 cloves
- 4-6 cardamom pods, lightly crushed
- 1 tsp cumin seeds
- 1 medium onion, sliced
- 1 green chilli, chopped
- 1 tbsp chopped ginger
- 2 garlic cloves, chopped
- 200g (7oz) long-grain rice, rinsed and drained
- 200g (7oz) chopped mixed vegetables
- 1 tbsp finely chopped coriander

METHOD

- Heat the oil in a pan over a medium heat. Add the bay leaf, cinnamon, cloves, cardamom, and cumin seeds, and fry until dark and fragrant.

- Add the onion, chilli, ginger, and garlic and cook, stirring continuously for 3–4 minutes.

- Add 600ml (1pint) water, increase the heat to high, and add the rice and vegetables. Bring the mixture to a boil. Cook until almost all the water is absorbed.

- Reduce the heat to low and cover the rice with a damp kitchen towel. Cover with a lid and cook until the rice is cooked through. Serve hot, garnished with coriander, with any raita of your choice.

BBQ CHICKEN

On a winter's day, you could cook this meal on an outdoor barbecue. The chicken also tastes good when cooked in a grill, as it's the marinade that gives it flavour.

1

Place all the ingredients, except the chicken drumsticks, in a bowl and whisk them together. Pour the mixture into a large, shallow dish.

2

Pat the chicken pieces with kitchen towels. Make 3 deep cuts in each drumstick. This is called scoring. It helps the meat to soak the marinade.

3

Place the chicken in the marinade and roll each piece until it is coated. Cover the dish with cling film and leave in the fridge for 1 hour. Preheat the oven to 180°C (350°F/Gas 4).

4

Lay the coated chicken (uncut side up) on a foil-lined grill pan. Put the marinade to one side. Bake the chicken for 20–25 minutes and baste it with marinade halfway through.

5

Turn off the oven and turn the grill on. Baste the chicken pieces and finish cooking them off under the grill for 8–10 minutes.

6

Using tongs, turn the chicken over halfway through grilling and baste it with marinade. This helps to keep it moist.

CHEESY HERBY MACARONI

Cozy up with a warm, cheesy bowl of this comforting macaroni, and you will feel better almost instantly! If you don't have Cheddar, try any cheese you like.

INGREDIENTS

- 225g (8oz) macaroni
- salt
- 60g (2oz) butter
- 1½ tbsp all-purpose flour
- 750ml (1¼ pints) milk
- 4 tbsp finely chopped flat-leaf parsley
- 4 tbsp finely chopped coriander
- 175g (6oz) shredded Cheddar cheese

TOOLS

- large saucepan
- ladle
- frying pan
- jug
- chopping board
- knife
- whisk
- colander
- spatula
- grater

1

Ask an adult to preheat the oven to 180°C (350°F/Gas 4). Cook the macaroni in a large saucepan of boiling salted water for 8–10 minutes. Drain well and set aside.

2

In a frying pan, melt the butter over medium heat. Add the flour and stir for a few minutes. Add salt to taste.

3

Slowly whisk in the milk. Cook until it turns into a thick and smooth sauce, whisking continuously. Stir in the parsley and coriander.

4

Remove the sauce from heat and stir in 115g (4oz) of the cheese until well combined and melted.

5

Add the macaroni to the sauce and mix well. Transfer to a deep ovenproof dish. Sprinkle over the remaining cheese.

6

Place the dish in the oven, and bake for 8–10 minutes until the cheese is browned and bubbling.

LAMB HOTPOT

This hotpot is a hearty main meal that will fill you up. The lamb and tomatoes make it juicy and the chickpeas add texture. Serve it with crusty bread rolls.

Serves 6 | Prep 25 mins | Cook 20 mins

1

Put the lamb, flour, and paprika into a mixing bowl and combine well so that the lamb is coated.

2

Heat the oil in a large pan over medium heat. Add the onion and cook for 5 minutes, stirring often. Add the lamb and cook until browned.

3

Stir in the garlic and chickpeas, and cook for one minute. Add the tomatoes, bring to the boil, then simmer for 15 minutes.

4

Season well with salt and black pepper, stir in the spinach, and cook for 3 minutes. Serve hot.

INGREDIENTS

- 175g (6oz) lean lamb, leg or fillet, cut into 2cm (³⁄₄in) diced
- ½ tbsp plain flour
- ¼ tsp paprika
- 1½ tbsp olive oil
- ½ large red onion, sliced
- 2 garlic cloves, chopped
- ½ 400g can chickpeas, drained and rinsed
- 400g can chopped tomatoes
- salt and freshly ground black pepper
- 125g (4½oz) baby leaf spinach

TOOLS

- large glass bowl
- large pan
- wooden spoon
- 6 bowls or individual casserole dishes to serve the hotpot in

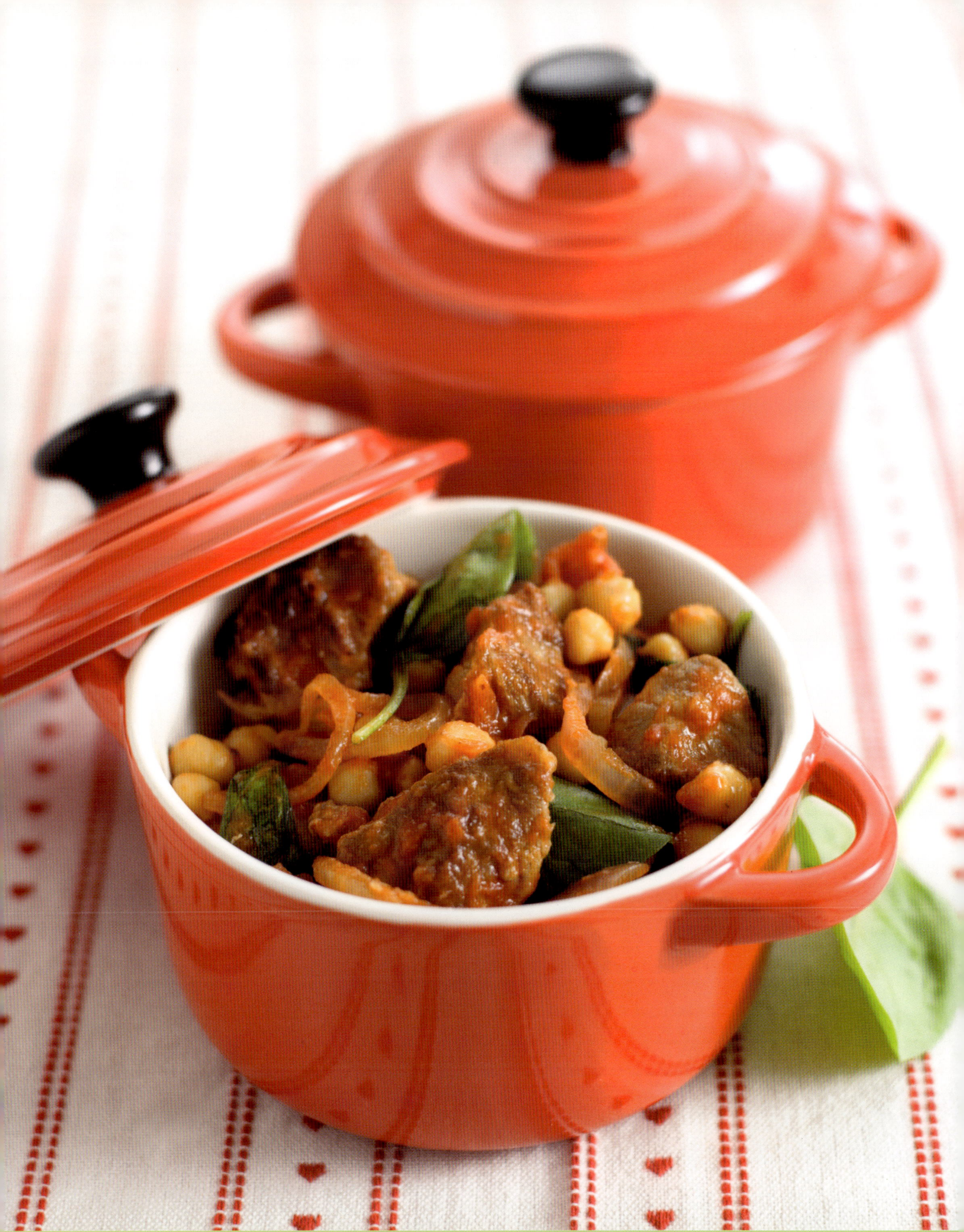

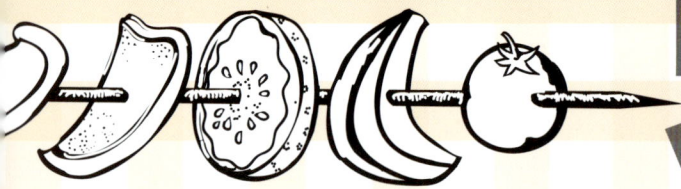

Kebabs are fun and really easy to make.

1

CHICKEN SATAY

This is a popular kebab recipe. Always soak the wooden skewers in cold water for 30 minutes to prevent them from burning.

INGREDIENTS

This recipe is for 4 people. It takes 20 minutes to prepare and 16 minutes to cook.

• 500g (1lb 2oz) chicken breasts

• ½ lime, cut into wedges, to serve

• Follow the recipe on page 34 for the satay sauce

METHOD

• Make the satay sauce in a large bowl and set aside. Save a small amount to use as a dip.

• Cut the chicken breasts into large chunks 4cm (1½in) cubes and place into the bowl of satay sauce. Marinate in the fridge for 1 hour.

• Thread the chicken chunks onto short skewers (or large skewers cut in half). Discard any remaining marinade.

• Place the kebabs on a grill pan and cook for about 8 minutes. Turn over and cook for another 8 minutes. Serve the chicken warm with the satay sauce for dipping and wedges of lime.

2

INGREDIENTS

This recipe is for 4 people. It takes 80 minutes to prepare and 20 minutes to cook.

For the marinade

• 2 tbsp olive oil

• 1 tbsp soy sauce

• 3 tbsp black bean sauce

• 1 tbsp clear runny honey

• 2 garlic cloves, crushed

For the kebabs

• 250g (9oz) firm tofu

• salt and freshly ground pepper

• 2 small courgettes, each cut into 8 wedges

• 2 medium red onions, cut into 8 wedges

• 1 medium red pepper, deseeded and cut into 16 chunks

TOFU CHUNKS

This colourful kebab would make a perfect vegetarian option for a summer barbecue.

METHOD

• Cut the tofu into 16 cubes. Put the cubes into a dish with the courgettes, onions, and red pepper.

• Mix the ingredients for the marinade in a large dish. Season. Use a spoon to coat the tofu and vegetables in the marinade. Put in the fridge for 1 hour.

• Thread the vegetables and tofu onto 8 skewers.

• Place the kebabs on the grill and brush them with the marinade. Grill for 15–20 minutes, turning them halfway through and brushing them with more marinade.

Yellow courgette

Mushrooms

Onions

Halloumi cheese

Aubergine

3

LAMB WITH MINT YOGURT

Lamb is delicious when flavoured with herbs and spices. To make the dip, mix grated cucumber, plain yogurt, and dried mint together. Season with salt and pepper.

INGREDIENTS

This recipe is for 4 people. It takes 20 minutes to prepare and 20 minutes to cook.

- 450g (1lb) minced lamb
- 1 small onion, finely chopped
- 1 garlic clove
- ½ tsp ground cinnamon
- 2 tsp ground cumin
- 1 tsp ground coriander
- olive oil, for brushing
- 1 tsp dried mint
- ½ lemon, to serve

METHOD

• Put the lamb mince in a mixing bowl. Add the chopped onion, garlic, cinnamon, cumin, and coriander to the bowl. Stir the ingredients until they are all combined.

• Divide the lamb mixture into 12 parts. Shape each one into a sausage and then thread them onto the skewers. Press or roll to lengthen the kebabs.

• Place the lamb kebabs onto the baking tray and brush them with oil. Grill them for about 5 minutes on each side, until golden. Transfer to a serving dish and sprinkle with mint.

4

PRAWN AND PEPPERS

This bright and colourful kebab is full of flavour. Squeeze lime juice on them to serve.

INGREDIENTS

This recipe is for 4 people. It takes 25 minutes to prepare and 15 minutes to cook.

For the marinade

- juice of 1 lemon
- 2 tbsp soy sauce
- 1 garlic clove, crushed
- 1 tsp light brown sugar

For the kebab

- ½ red pepper
- ½ yellow pepper
- 4 baby sweetcorn
- 8 cherry tomatoes
- 150g (5½oz) cooked prawns

METHOD

• Make the marinade by mixing the ingredients together in a jug. Carefully cut the peppers and baby sweetcorn into chunks

• Thread the vegetables and prawns onto the skewers. Place the kebabs into a rectangular dish. Pour the marinade over them. Put the kebabs into the fridge for 1 hour. Turn them over after 30 minutes.

• Grill the kebabs for 15 minutes. Baste the prawns every five minutes with the marinade (discard any leftover marinade).

CHICKEN TIKKA MASALA

India's most famous international dish, chicken tikka masala requires some time to prepare, but the rich, creamy result is well worth the effort.

INGREDIENTS

For the marinade
- 2 tbsp ginger-garlic paste
- ½ tsp salt
- ½ tsp red chilli powder
- juice of 1 lemon
- 60g (2oz) plain yogurt, plus extra for garnishing
- 900g (2lb) chicken breast, boneless and cut into 2.5cm (1in) pieces
- 2 tbsp vegetable oil

For the sauce
- 2 tbsp butter or *ghee*
- 2 garlic cloves, minced
- 2 tbsp curry powder
- 1 tsp paprika
- 3 tbsp tomato paste (optional)
- 250ml (9fl oz) tomato purée or pulp
- 250ml (9fl oz) heavy cream
- salt, to taste
- coriander, to garnish
- basmati rice, to serve

TOOLS
- bowl
- spoon
- grilling pan
- large skillet
- wooden spatula

1

In a mixing bowl, combine the ginger-garlic paste, salt, chilli powder, lemon juice, and yogurt. Add the chicken and mix until evenly coated.

2

Cover the bowl with cling film and leave in the fridge for 4 hours or overnight.

3

Heat the oil in a grilling pan and grill the chicken over medium-high heat for 10 minutes or until it is cooked and tender. This can be done in your oven's broiler as well.

4

For the sauce, melt the butter or *ghee* in a large skillet over medium heat. Add the garlic, curry powder, paprika, tomato paste, tomato purée or pulp, and 120ml (4fl oz) water. Bring to the boil.

Reduce the heat, then add the cream, chicken, and salt. Simmer for 3–4 minutes until well blended. Garnish with coriander and serve hot with basmati rice.

BEETROOT RAITA

A lovely pink in colour, this raita not only looks pretty, but is also very healthy. It goes well with any rice dish.

Serves 6 | Prep 10 mins | Cook 30 mins

1

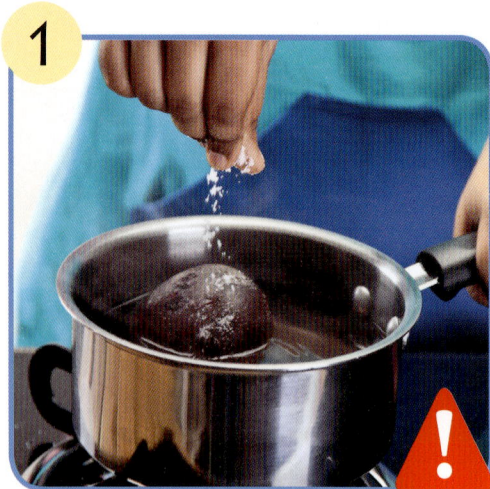

In a small pan, combine the beetroot, 500ml (16fl oz) water, and salt and bring to the boil over high heat.

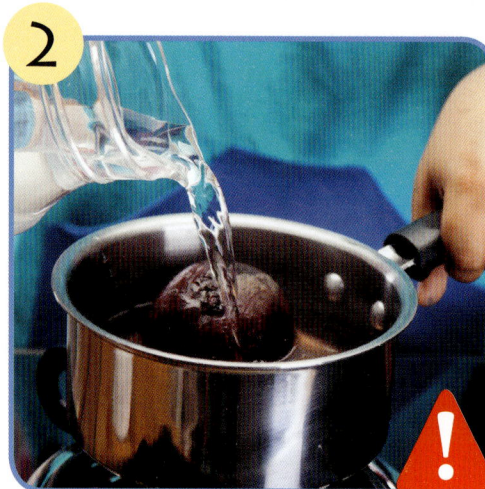

2

Add more water, if required, and continue to cook until the beet is cooked through.

3

Remove from the heat and let it cool. Peel and cut the beet into 1cm (½in) cubes.

4

Gently whisk the yogurt with the green chilli, lime juice, and sugar until smooth. Add salt to taste. Mix in the chopped beets and serve chilled, garnished with the coriander.

INGREDIENTS

- 1 medium beetroot
- 500g (1lb 2oz) plain yogurt
- 1 green chilli, finely chopped
- juice of 1 lime
- 1 tbsp sugar
- salt
- a few sprigs of coriander, to garnish

TOOLS

- boiling pan
- peeler
- knife
- bowl
- whisk
- spoon

DID YOU KNOW?

Beetroot leaves are also edible and can be cooked like spinach or mustard. It was believed that the beetroot was grown in the Hanging Gardens of Babylon and offered to the Sun God Apollo.

FISHCAKES

Potatoes can be cooked in many ways – mashed, boiled, roasted, and baked. Bite into these crunchy fishcakes, and the creamy fish and mash will melt in your mouth.

TOP TIP

The recipe works great with any white-fleshed fish. Adding finely chopped garlic and fresh coriander will give the dish a new twist.

INGREDIENTS

- 250g (9oz) undyed smoked haddock, trimmed
- 1 fresh bay leaf
- 300ml (10fl oz) milk
- 375g (¾lb) potatoes, peeled and mashed
- 8 spring onions, finely chopped
- 100g (3½oz) can sweetcorn
- 4 eggs, hard-boiled, peeled, and chopped
- 2 tbsp chopped flat-leaf parsley
- zest of 1 lemon
- 120g (4oz) double cream
- 2 egg yolks, plus 2 eggs
- 100g (3½oz) flour
- 125g (4½oz) breadcrumbs (see page 11 for instructions)
- 1 tbsp butter
- 2 tbsp olive oil
- salsa, to serve
- lemon wedges, to serve

TOOLS

- shallow pan
- large mixing bowl
- fork
- spoon
- 2 small glass bowls
- whisk
- chopping board
- large shallow bowl
- large plate
- frying pan
- spatula

1

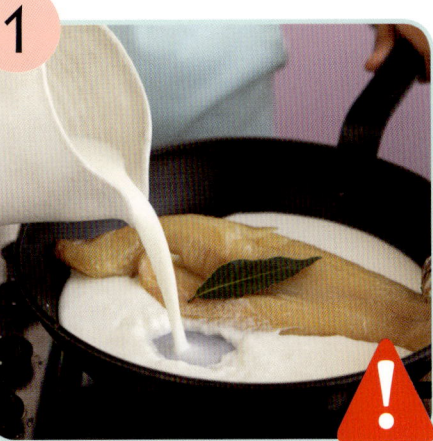

Cook the fillets with the bay leaf and the milk in a shallow pan. Simmer for 5–10 minutes. Cool, then remove the fish's skin and any bones, and flake into chunks.

2

Mix the fish, potatoes, spring onions, sweetcorn, chopped eggs, parsley, and lemon zest. In a small bowl, beat the cream with the egg yolks, and stir into the mixture.

3

Divide the mixture into four parts. Shape each part into a slightly flattened ball. Roll each fishcake in the flour on a plate. Shake off any excess.

4

Crack two eggs into a small bowl and whisk. Transfer to a large, shallow bowl. Dip each fishcake into the eggs so that they get egg all over the surface.

5

Dip the egg-coated fishcake into the breadcrumbs and coat all over, then set aside. Repeat dipping into eggs, then breadcrumbs with the remaining fishcakes.

6

Heat the oil and butter in a frying pan and add the fishcakes carefully. Cook them gently for about 4–5 minutes on each side, or until golden-brown.

JAMBALAYA

This is a colourful Creole or Cajun rice dish from Louisiana in the USA. It's simple to make because all the ingredients are cooked in the same pot.

INGREDIENTS

- 250g (9oz) brown rice
- 1 large onion, chopped
- 3 skinless chicken breasts
- 200g (7oz) smoked ham
- 2 tbsp olive oil
- 2 large garlic cloves, chopped
- 1 red pepper, deseeded and cut into bite-sized pieces
- 1 green chilli, deseeded and finely chopped (optional)
- 1 tsp paprika
- 1 tsp dried thyme
- 700ml (1¼ pints) warm chicken or vegetable stock
- 3 tbsp can chopped tomatoes
- 50g (1¾oz) peas
- salt

TOOLS

- sieve
- small sharp knife
- chopping board
- large saucepan with lid
- wooden spoon

1 Put the rice in a sieve and rinse it under cold water until the water runs clear. Washing the rice before cooking prevents the grains of rice from sticking together.

2 Chop the onion into small pieces and set aside. Carefully cut the chicken and ham into bite-sized pieces. Heat the oil in a large saucepan.

3 Fry the chicken and onion for 8 minutes over medium heat until the chicken is golden all over. Stir frequently so it doesn't stick to the pan.

4 Add the ham, garlic, red pepper, and chilli, and cook for 2 minutes. Add the paprika, thyme, rice, stock, tomatoes and peas. Stir and bring to the boil.

5

Reduce the heat to low. Cover the pan and simmer for 35 minutes or until the rice is cooked and the water is absorbed. Season the rice with salt and stir before serving.

MARINATED LIME CHICKEN

The zingy lime and fresh coriander leaves give this dish a delicious combination of refreshing flavours. Serve with potatoes and your choice of vegetables.

Serves 4 · **Prep 80 mins** · **Cook 30 mins**

INGREDIENTS

- 4 skinless chicken breasts
- 2 eggs
- 175g (6oz) of breadcrumbs
- 4 tbsp sunflower oil, for frying
- potatoes and beans, to serve

For the marinade
- juice of 4 limes, plus 1 lime, finely sliced
- handful of chopped fresh coriander
- 2 garlic cloves, peeled and finely sliced

TOOLS
- knife
- large bowls
- spoon
- cling film
- frying pan
- spatula

1 Carefully make four small cuts on the top of each chicken breast to help marinate flavour into the meat.

2 Make the marinade by mixing all the ingredients in a bowl. Place the chicken in the marinade. Cover the bowl with cling film and chill for 1 hour in the fridge.

3 Beat the eggs in a bowl and place one piece of chicken in the bowl. Turn the chicken breast so it gets covered in egg.

4 Coat the chicken breast in breadcrumbs. Repeat steps 3 and 4 for each piece of chicken. Discard any remaining marinade.

5 Fry the chicken in oil on medium heat for 10–15 minutes on each side. Chicken needs to be cooked through with no sign of pink.

TOP TIP

Add fresh, finely chopped ginger in the marinade. It adds a wonderful flavour to the chicken.

VEGETABLE TART

This dish is best served cold. It's perfect for a light evening meal or lunch. Try it with some potato salad and a green salad.

6 Serves 6 | **135 mins** Prep | **65 mins** Cook

TOOLS

- sieve
- mixing bowl
- knife
- fork
- tablespoon
- cling film
- rolling pin
- flan tin, loose-bottomed and fluted, approx. 20cm (8in) diameter
- table knife
- greaseproof paper
- baking beans or dried kidney beans
- oven gloves
- jug
- whisk

INGREDIENTS

- 225g (8oz) plain flour, plus extra for rolling
- a pinch of salt
- 90g (3oz) unsalted butter, diced, plus extra for greasing
- 30g (1oz) vegetable fat or lard, cubed
- 100g (3½oz) red pepper, deseeded and diced
- 125g (4½oz) sweetcorn
- 125g (4½oz) peas
- 1 small leek, sliced and sautéed
- 2 eggs, beaten
- 100ml (3½fl oz) milk
- 100ml (3½fl oz) cream
- 30g (1oz) Cheddar cheese, grated

1

Sift the flour and salt into a bowl. Stir in the butter and fat until coated with flour. Rub the fats into the flour.

2

Once the mixture looks like crumbs, add 2 tablespoons of water, drop by drop, and stir with a knife. When the crumbs start to come together, gather the pastry in your hands.

3

Shape the pastry into a smooth disc and wrap it in cling film. Chill it for 1 hour in the fridge or until firm. Grease your tin and lightly flour your work top.

4

Roll out the pastry so that it is slightly bigger than the tin. Gently press it into the tin and use a knife to trim off the excess. Use a fork to prick the base and chill it again for 15 minutes. Ask an adult to preheat the oven to 200°C (400°F/Gas 6).

5

Cover the tart with 2 layers of greaseproof paper. Add the baking beans. Bake for 15 minutes, remove the paper and beans, and bake for a further 5 minutes. This is called baking blind and it helps the pastry stay firm when the wet filling is added.

6

Turn the oven down to 180°C (350°F/Gas 4). Scatter the vegetables over the base. Whisk the eggs, milk, and cream together and pour into the tart. Sprinkle over the cheese and bake for 45 minutes. Allow the tart to set and cool before serving.

SWEET TREATS

MINT CHOCOLATE POTS

These luxury, rather grown-up, desserts are super-chocolatey but with a minty kick. Dress them up with a stencilled shape of icing sugar or cocoa.

Serves 4 | **Prep 45 mins** | **Cook 45-60 mins**

INGREDIENTS

- 300ml (10fl oz) double cream
- small bunch of chopped mint
- 120ml (4fl oz) milk
- 175g (6oz) milk chocolate, broken into small pieces
- 3 egg yolks
- 1 tbsp icing sugar, plus extra for dusting
- cocoa powder, for dusting (optional)

TOOLS

- chopping board
- sharp knife
- 2 saucepans
- mixing bowl
- wooden spoon
- whisk
- sieve
- roasting tin
- 4 ramekins
- card, pencil, scissors for decoration

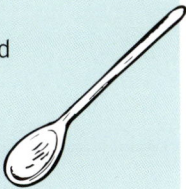

1

Ask an adult to preheat the oven to 150°C (300°F/Gas 2). Pour the cream into a small pan and add the mint. Heat gently until nearly boiling, then remove from heat, cover, and leave for 30 minutes.

2

Meanwhile, pour the milk into another small pan and heat gently. Remove from the heat and stir in the chocolate pieces until melted and the mixture is smooth.

3

Whisk the egg yolks and sugar together and add the chocolatey milk and the minty cream. Mix well, then strain the mixture through a fine sieve to remove the mint.

4

Pour the mixture into 4 ramekins stood in a roasting tin. Add hot water until it's halfway up the outside of the cups. Bake for 45–60 minutes. Let them cool and then refrigerate for a few hours. Decorate with icing sugar and cocoa powder just before serving, if you want.

Whether you go for delicately or boldly decorated cupcakes, make sure you have enough toppings to choose from. Tie in with a theme if they're for a party.

INGREDIENTS

- 150g (5½oz) unsalted butter, softened
- 150g (5½oz) caster sugar
- 150g (5½oz) self-raising flour
- 3 eggs, whisked
- ½ tsp vanilla extract

For icing and decoration

- 225g (8oz) icing sugar, sifted
- 3 different food colourings
- edible crystallized flowers, sugar strands, hundreds and thousands, or sweets

TOOLS

- 2 x 12-hole bun tins
- 20 paper cases
- 5 mixing bowls
- wooden spoon
- 2 metal spoons
- cooling rack
- sieve
- knife

1

Line 2 bun tins with 20 paper cases – there are plenty of different designs to choose from. Ask an adult to preheat the oven to 180°C (350°F/Gas 4).

2

Place the butter, sugar, flour, eggs, and vanilla extract in a bowl. Mix with a wooden spoon until pale in colour and creamy.

3

Divide between the paper cases. Bake for 15 minutes until golden and just firm. Let the cupcakes cool in the tin for 5 minutes, then transfer to a cooling rack.

4

Trim any pointed tops to make a flat surface. This will allow the icing to sit better. The cupcakes are now ready for your decorations.

5

Mix the icing sugar in a large bowl. Gradually beat in 2–3 tablespoons of hot water to give a smooth thick icing, which coats the back of a spoon.

6

Transfer the icing mixture to 3 individual bowls and add a few drops of food colouring to each. Spoon onto the cakes and top with decorations. Allow to set.

STRAWBERRY TARTS

These pretty pastries taste as good as they look! You can also make them with other types of soft fruit.

8 Makes 8 | **20 mins** Prep | **14 mins** Cook

INGREDIENTS

- 225g (8oz) ready-made shortcrust pastry
- 150g (5½oz) mascarpone cheese
- ½ tsp vanilla extract
- 2 tbsp icing sugar
- 175g (6oz) strawberries or other soft fruit
- 4 tbsp redcurrant jelly

TOOLS

- rolling pin
- 9cm (3½in) fluted cutter
- 12-hole bun tin
- baking parchment
- dried beans or chickpeas
- oven gloves
- cooling rack
- small mixing bowl
- wooden spoon
- sieve
- chopping board
- sharp knife
- teaspoon
- small saucepan
- pastry brush
- frying pan
- spatula

1

Preheat the oven to 200°C (400°F/Gas 6). Thinly roll out the pastry, then using a fluted cutter, cut out 8 circles. Press the pastry circles into a bun tin.

2

Line the cases with baking parchment and fill them with dried beans. Cook for 10 minutes, then remove the beans. Return to the oven for 3 minutes. Cool in the tin.

3

Transfer the cases to a cooling rack. Place the cheese and vanilla extract in a mixing bowl. Sift over the icing sugar, then beat with a wooden spoon until smooth.

4

Place the strawberries on a chopping board. Remove the green stalks from the strawberries. Then, use a knife to cut them in half or quarters if they are large.

5

When the pastry cases are completely cool, use a teaspoon to fill them with the mascarpone and vanilla mixture. Arrange the strawberries over the top.

6

Place the redcurrant jelly in a small pan with 1 tablespoon water and cook over low heat, stirring until the jelly has dissolved. Brush this over the strawberries.

Ingredients

- 350g (12oz) plain flour
- 2 tsp ground ginger
- 1 tsp bicarbonate of soda
- 125g (4½oz) butter, diced
- 150g (5½oz) soft dark brown sugar
- 4 tbsp golden syrup
- 1 egg, beaten
- sweets, currants, and icing, for decoration

Tools

- 2 large baking trays
- baking parchment
- large mixing bowl
- wooden spoon
- rolling pin
- cutters of your choice
- oven gloves

GINGERBREAD

Fill your house with the wondrous smell of baking gingerbread. Search out some unusual cutters to make your shapes stand out from the crowd.

Makes 15 | Prep 15 mins | Cook 10 mins

1

Ask an adult to preheat the oven to 180°C (350°F/Gas 4). Line 2 large baking trays with baking parchment. If you only have 1 tray, you will need to cook the biscuits in a couple of batches.

2

Place the flour, ginger, and bicarbonate of soda in a large bowl. Stir the ingredients together with a wooden spoon until they are thoroughly mixed.

3

Rub the butter into the mixture using your fingertips. Continue rubbing in the butter until the mixture resembles fine breadcrumbs. Stir in the sugar.

4

Stir in the golden syrup and egg until the mixture starts to come together in a dough. Next, tip the dough mixture out onto a lightly floured surface and knead it until smooth.

5

Roll out the dough on a lightly floured surface to a thickness of 5mm (¼in), then using your cutters, cut out the shapes. Re-roll the leftover dough and cut out more biscuits until it's all used.

6

Place the biscuits on the baking trays and bake in the oven for 9–10 minutes or until golden. Allow the biscuits to cool on the trays. Decorate with sweets, currants, and icing.

CARROT & ORANGE MUFFINS

The versatile carrot can be savoury or sweet, as in these delicious muffins – a perfect snack or lunch box treat.

INGREDIENTS

- 140g (5oz) plain flour
- 2 tsp baking powder
- ½ tsp bicarbonate of soda
- 85g (3oz) light brown sugar
- 50g (1¾oz) roasted hazelnuts, chopped
- 100g (3½oz) carrot, grated
- 100g (3½oz) unsulphured apricots, finely chopped
- 1 tbsp poppy seeds
- ½ tsp ground cinnamon
- 100g (3½oz) porridge oats
- zest of 2 oranges
- 200ml (7fl oz) buttermilk
- 1 egg, beaten
- 3 tbsp melted butter
- a pinch of salt
- juice of 1 large orange

For the topping
- 2 tbsp soft brown sugar
- 50g (1¾oz) porridge oats
- 1 tbsp melted butter

TOOLS

- small glass bowl
- baking tray
- chopping board
- sharp knife
- large glass bowl
- spoon
- muffin cases
- muffin tray

1

Ask an adult to preheat the oven to 200°C (400°F/Gas 6). For the topping, mix together the ingredients in a bowl. Sprinkle the mixture onto a baking tray. Bake for 5 minutes, then leave to cool.

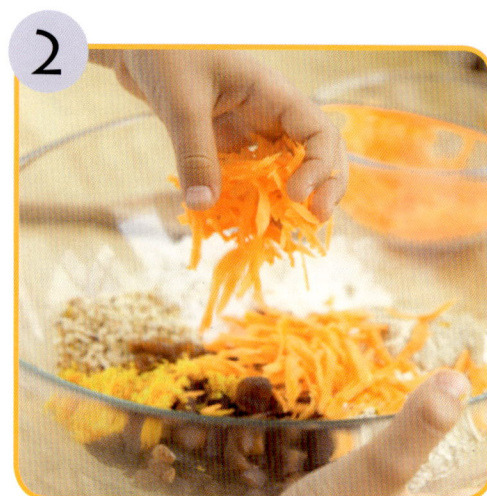

2

In a large bowl, mix the flour, baking powder, bicarbonate of soda, and sugar. Then, add the nuts, carrot, apricots, poppy seeds, cinnamon, oats, and orange zest. Mix together well.

3

In another bowl, use a spoon to mix the buttermilk, egg, butter, salt, and orange juice. Pour this liquid mixture onto the bowl of dry ingredients.

4

Stir the two mixtures together using a spoon. Be careful not to over mix as this will "knock out" all the air. In fact, the lumpier the mixture, the better the muffins.

5

Place 8 paper cases into a muffin tray. Spoon the mixture into the cases, filling them two-thirds.

6

⚠️

Sprinkle the crumbly topping over the muffins. Bake in the oven for about 25–30 minutes until well risen and golden. Leave to cool.

FOUR WAYS WITH COOKIES

Everyone enjoys making cookies and everyone loves to eat them. Try out these tasty combinations or come up with your own.

1

2

TRADITIONAL CHOCOLATE

This is a classic cookie that everyone likes. Why not try chunks of milk chocolate or chunks of white chocolate instead? You could add a twist to this cookie by adding nuts.

INGREDIENTS

(to add to the dough recipe above)

- 75g (2½oz) dark chocolate, broken into small pieces

METHOD

- Make the chunks quite big so that they are nice and gooey when you bite into a cookie.

- On a cold day, you could make hot chocolate to serve with the cookies for a real chocolatey treat.

APRICOTS & CINNAMON

There are other spices you can try instead of cinnamon. Put a quarter of a teaspoon of mixed spice or an eighth of a teaspoon of ground ginger. You can substitute apricots for raisins or sultanas

INGREDIENTS

(to add to the basic dough recipe above)

- 75g (2½oz) dried apricots, finely chopped
- ¼ tsp ground cinnamon

METHOD

- Make the apricot pieces small so that they are scattered well throughout each cookie.

- Store in a tin for a couple of days, if they don't get eaten before then!

1

Preheat the oven to 180°C (350°F/Gas 4). Line two trays with baking parchment. In a large bowl, using an electric whisk, whisk the butter and egg together. Mix in the sugar and vanilla extract.

2

Work in the flour with a spoon until the mixture forms a soft dough, then mix in your additional ingredients from one of the recipes below. Chill in the fridge for 30 minutes.

3

Roll the dough into 16 balls and place on the baking trays, leaving space around each. Flatten the balls slightly and bake in the oven for 15 minutes or until golden. Cool them on a wire rack.

3

HAZELNUT DELIGHTS

Hazelnuts have a brilliant flavour and crunch. Alternatively, you could try the same quantity of another nut. Do you like peanuts, walnuts, pecans, or pistachios?

INGREDIENTS

(to add to the basic dough recipe above)

• 75g (2½oz) hazelnuts, cut in half

METHOD

• Toast the nuts under the grill for 2 minutes before you stir them into the dough mixture.

• Wrap up a pile of cookies in baking parchment and tie it with ribbon to make a parcel to give to someone.

4

CRANBERRY CHEWS

You can play around with trying the same quantity of another dried fruit. Which is your favourite? Try raisins, mangoes, apples, blueberries, or cherries.

INGREDIENTS

(to add to the basic dough recipe above)

• 45g (1½oz) white chocolate, broken into small pieces

• 45g (1½oz) dried cranberries, finely chopped

METHOD

• Mix the ingredients really well so that the cranberries and white chocolate don't all sit together. They need to be spread out well in each cookie.

• Serve the cookies with a glass of milk for each person.

BROWNIES

A real crowd-pleasing treat, brownies taste divine whether made with white, milk, or plain chocolate. If you're feeling hungry, just cut them into larger pieces and share out.

16 Makes 16

25 mins Prep

25 mins Cook

INGREDIENTS

- 150g (5½oz) unsalted butter, diced, plus extra for greasing
- 90g (3oz) plain chocolate
- 125g (4½oz) plain flour
- 15g (½oz) cocoa powder
- ½ tsp baking powder
- a pinch of salt
- 2 eggs
- 300g (10oz) soft, light brown sugar
- 1 tsp vanilla extract
- 100g (3½oz) pecan nuts, chopped (optional)

TOOLS

- baking tin 20 x 15cm (8 x 6in)
- scissors
- pencil
- baking parchment
- 3 medium bowls
- wooden spoon
- small saucepan
- sieve
- spatula
- palette knife
- oven gloves

1

Grease and line the base of the baking tin with baking parchment. Ask an adult to preheat the oven to 180°C (350°F/Gas 4).

2

Break the chocolate into a bowl and add the chunks of butter. Melt the butter and chocolate over a pan of barely simmering water, stirring occasionally.

3

Remove the bowl from the heat and allow the chocolate to cool slightly. In a separate bowl, sieve the flour, cocoa powder, baking powder, and salt.

4

In a third bowl, beat the eggs and then add the sugar and vanilla extract. Stir the ingredients together until they are just combined.

5

Fold the melted chocolate into the beaten egg mixture using a spatula. Then fold in the flour mixture and nuts, if using. You shouldn't be able to see any flour once it's mixed.

6

Spoon the mixture into the tin, smooth the top with a palette knife, and bake for 25 minutes. Allow it to cool in the tin before cutting into squares.

FRIDGE CAKE

A no-cook cake, what could be easier? And you get to do some bashing. This cake uses nuts, but you could swap it for other types of dried fruit, such as cranberries, if you prefer.

Makes 24 | Prep 10 mins | Cook 1 hour

INGREDIENTS

- 450g (1lb) digestive biscuits
- 150g (5½oz) butter
- 500g (1lb 2oz) dark chocolate, broken into pieces
- 2 tbsp golden syrup
- 50g (1¾oz) raisins
- 50g (1¾oz) almonds, chopped

TOOLS

- rolling pin
- plastic bag
- mixing bowl
- saucepan
- wooden spoon
- 18 x 18cm (7 x 7in) tin
- baking parchment
- potato masher
- sharp knife
- chopping board

1

Place the biscuits in a plastic bag and bash them with a rolling pin. Don't break them too finely, though. You need chunks still, not dust.

2

Melt the butter, chocolate, and syrup in a bowl over a saucepan of hot water. Stir together to make a shiny mixture. Remove from the heat.

3

When the bowl is cool to touch, stir in the biscuits, raisins, and almonds. Make sure all the ingredients are mixed really well. Now, line the tin with baking parchment.

4

Use a masher to press the mixture into the tin and put in the fridge to harden. Cut into 24 pieces. If you like, freeze some in an airtight container and eat within a few months.

BANANA FRITTERS

These bananas are cooked in a light batter, coated with sesame seeds, and served with a delicious warm fudge sauce.

Makes 4 · Prep 20 mins · Cook 15 mins

INGREDIENTS

- 4 bananas, peeled and cut into 4 pieces
- sunflower oil, for frying

For the fudge sauce
- 75g (2½oz) unsalted butter
- 150g (5½ oz) light soft brown sugar
- 150ml (5fl oz) cream
- 1 tbsp golden syrup

For the batter
- 125g (4½oz) self-raising flour
- 2 tbsp caster sugar
- 175ml (6fl oz) milk
- 4 tbsp sesame seeds

TOOLS

- large saucepan
- wooden spoon
- large bowl
- large metal spoon
- teaspoon
- slotted spoon
- kitchen paper

1 Place all the fudge sauce ingredients in a pan and cook gently for 2–3 minutes. Stirring continuously, bring to the boil for 3 minutes until thickened.

2 Leave in the pan to cool slightly. Meanwhile, heat another pan one-third full of oil, until a piece of bread goes golden-brown when dropped in.

3 Mix all the batter ingredients together in a large bowl, reserving 2 tablespoons of the sesame seeds. Add the bananas and turn to coat in the batter.

4 Using a slotted spoon, and holding over the bowl, remove the bananas, then sprinkle with some of the reserved sesame seeds.

5

Fry the banana in batches in the oil for 3–4 minutes until golden-brown. Remove and drain on kitchen paper. Serve immediately with the fudge sauce.

TOP TIP

Add cinnamon and nutmeg for warm flavours and wonderful aroma.

MANGO POPS

These fruity ice pops are made from pure fruit purée. Decorate with a little melted chocolate and hundreds and thousands.

Makes 8 | Prep 20 mins | Freezing 6 hours

⭐

INGREDIENTS

- 2 large ripe mangoes
- 2 tbsp icing sugar
- juice of 1 lime
- 150g (5½oz) plain or milk chocolate, broken into pieces
- 50g (1¾oz) hundreds and thousands

TOOLS

- knife
- chopping board
- food processor
- ice lolly moulds
- 8 sticks

1

To dice the mangoes, copy step 3 on page 29. Place the mango in a food processor with the icing sugar and lime juice and blend to a smooth purée.

2

Pour into 8 moulds and put the sticks in. Freeze for 6 hours. Melt the chocolate and dip the pops in, then dip in the hundreds and thousands. Keep in the freezer until ready to serve.

VERY BERRY JELLY

These individual jellies are made using a mixture of frozen berries. Alternatively, you could just use one type of berry, such as frozen raspberries or blueberries.

4 — Makes 4
5 mins — Prep
3 hours — Setting

1

Place the jelly into a measuring jug and pour over 300ml (½ pint) boiling water. Stir until the jelly has dissolved.

2

Stir the fruit into the jug. Top up with cold water to make 600ml (1 pint), if necessary.

INGREDIENTS
- 135g (5oz) pack of raspberry or blackcurrant flavour jelly
- 150g (5½oz) mixed frozen berries

TOOLS
- heatproof jug
- spoon
- jelly moulds

3

Spoon the mixture between one large jelly mould or four individual moulds and keep in the fridge for about 3 hours until set.

APPLE CRUMBLE SUNDAE

Apple, crunchy crumble, toffee sauce, and ice cream are layered up in tall glasses to make this delicious sundae.

Serves 4 | Prep 15 mins | Cook 15 mins

INGREDIENTS

For crumble mixture
- 100g (3½oz) plain flour
- 50g (1¾oz) butter, diced
- 50g (1¾oz) demerara sugar

For apple compote
- 3 cooking apples, peeled, cored and chopped
- 50g (1¾) caster sugar
- juice of ½ lemon
- 90ml (3fl oz) toffee sauce (see page 62)
- 8 scoops vanilla ice cream

TOOLS
- medium bowl
- baking tray
- baking parchment
- medium saucepan
- wooden spoon
- fork

1

Place the flour and butter in a bowl and rub them together with your fingertips until the mixture resembles fine breadcrumbs. Stir in the sugar.

2

Ask an adult to preheat the oven to 200°C (400°F/Gas 6). Line a baking tray with baking parchment and pour the mixture on top. Cook for 8–10 minutes until golden.

3

Meanwhile, place the apples, caster sugar, and lemon juice in a medium pan. Cover and cook over a gentle heat for 12–15 minutes, stirring occasionally.

4

Leave the apple compote to cool, with the lid off. Using your fingers or a fork, break up the cooled crumble topping.

5

Layer each sundae glass with apple compote, crumble, ice cream, and toffee sauce (see step 2, page 62) and serve with long spoons.

BLUEBERRY CHEESECAKE

These layered desserts look impressive but are easy-peasy to make. Making them in glasses means you can see the colourful layers.

Serves 4

10 mins — Prep

80 mins — Cook

1

Place three-quarters of the berries and half of the sugar into a small saucepan. Cover and simmer for 5 minutes until soft. Stir in the other berries and leave to cool.

2

Using a clean wooden spoon, beat the cream cheese, crème fraîche, remaining sugar, and vanilla extract together in a mixing bowl. Continue until well mixed and soft.

3

Create a layered look by filling 4 glasses with a spoonful of the blueberry sauce, then a spoonful of the cream cheese mixture, and then a spoonful of the crushed biscuits.

4

Repeat the layers once more and then put the filled glasses in the fridge for 1 hour to give the mixture time to set. Serve chilled straight from the fridge.

INGREDIENTS

- 500g (1lb 2oz) blueberries
- 2 tbsp caster sugar
- 250g (9oz) cream cheese
- 200ml (7fl oz) crème fraîche
- ¼ tbsp vanilla extract
- 8 oat biscuits, crushed

TOOLS

- small saucepan
- wooden spoon
- bowl
- dessert spoon
- 4 glasses

📎 **TOP TIP**

If blueberries aren't your fave, then you can simply use blackberries or raspberries instead. Whichever you choose, the finished result will still be a knockout!

125

ALMOND-CHOCOLATE BALLS

These little treats make a perfect post-dinner dessert. The sweet condensed milk makes them really rich and creamy.

Serves 4-6

4 hrs 15 mins
Prep

1

In a bowl, mix together the condensed milk, coconut, almonds, raisins, and cardamom. Shape the mixture into 2.5cm (1in) balls.

2

Place the balls on a tray and keep in the fridge for 3–4 hours.

3

Coat them lightly in drinking chocolate powder and serve.

INGREDIENTS

- 120ml (4fl oz) sweetened condensed milk
- 175g (6oz) desiccated coconut
- 30g (1oz) almonds, coarsely chopped
- 45g (1½oz) raisins
- 1 tsp ground cardamom seeds
- 30g (1oz) drinking chocolate powder

TOOLS

- bowl
- spoon
- tray

TOP TIP

Add fruit to give a natural sweetness and colour to the balls. Combining finely chopped strawberries, plums, blueberries, peaches, or any of your favourite seasonal fruit will not only surprise your guests, but also make this simple dish memorable.

5

Arrange the triangles on a serving plate and pour the thickened milk mixture over. Garnish with almonds and pistachios and serve immediately.

TOP TIP

This rich dish is a traditional Mughal dessert. Try using multigrain bread or any flavoured bread for your own version. You can also add vanilla or chocolate to the thick creamy sauce.

129

CREAMY PISTA ICE CREAM

A perfect treat on a stick for those long, hot summer holidays. The pistachios give the ice cream a cool, pale green colour.

1

Start with grinding the pistachios with a little condensed milk. Stir into the remaining condensed milk in a pan and bring it to the boil.

2

Add the cream and simmer over a medium heat for 10 minutes.

3

Stir in the sugar and salt, and cook for 5 minutes. Remove from heat and leave to cool.

4

Pour into moulds and freeze until firm.

INGREDIENTS

- 100g (3½oz) pistachios, finely ground
- 300ml (10fl oz) condensed milk
- 240ml (8fl oz) light cream
- 25g (scant 1oz) sugar
- a pinch of salt

SUGAR

TOOLS

- hand-blender
- pan
- spoon
- popsicle moulds

TOP TIP

Surprise your family and friends with this summer delight of soft, slushy ice cream. You can serve it in cones to add a little crunch to this treat.

CHOCOLATE TRUFFLES

Enough to bring a smile on anyone's face, chocolate truffles make a delicious gift. They can be stored in the fridge for up to a week – if only they last that long!

INGREDIENTS

- 100g (3½oz) bar of plain or milk chocolate
- 3 tbsp double cream
- ½ tsp vanilla extract
- 1 tbsp butter
- 2 tbsp cocoa powder
- 2 tbsp grated coconut

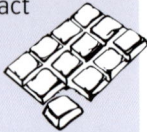

TOOLS

- bowl
- pan
- spoon
- plate
- card, plastic, and ribbon for decoration

DID YOU KNOW?

Swiss people eat more chocolate per head than people of any other nationality.

1

Snap the chocolate into a bowl. Add the cream, vanilla extract, and butter. Put the bowl over a pan of simmering water to melt the chocolate, stirring occasionally.

2

Let the chocolate mixture cool, then put it in the freezer. Stir every 5 minutes or so until the mixture is thick and fudgy.

3

For each truffle, roll a teaspoon of the fudge mixture into a ball in your hands (quickly so it doesn't melt). Then, roll it in cocoa powder or coconut.

4

For a special present, place a couple of truffles on a piece of card, wrap in plastic, and tie with ribbon.

TOP TIP

You can even use white or dark chocolate for a slightly different taste.

LEMON & LIME CAKE

The lemon and lime juice make this cake scrumptiously moist and full of flavour. The runny glacé icing adds an extra sweetness. Share it with your family and friends.

Serves 12 | Prep 15 mins | Cook 60 mins

1

Using an electric whisk, mix in the butter and caster sugar until light and fluffy. Line the loaf tin with baking parchment.

2

Beat in the eggs, a little at a time, then gently fold in the lemon and lime zest, together with one tablespoon of the lemon juice. Sift in the flour, then fold in with the poppy seeds, if using.

3

Transfer to the tin and smooth the top. Bake for 1 hour or until golden. Cool in the tin for 5 minutes, then move to a wire rack.

4

Mix the remaining lemon juice with the lime juice. Sift in the icing sugar and combine to make a runny icing. Spoon it over the cake.

INGREDIENTS

- 175g (6oz) butter, at room temperature
- 175g (6oz) caster sugar
- 3 large eggs
- grated zest of 1 lemon
- grated zest of 1 lime
- 2 tbsp lemon juice
- 175g (6oz) self-raising flour
- 2 tbsp poppy seeds (optional)
- 1 tbsp lime juice
- 100g (3oz) icing sugar

TOOLS

- electric whisk
- bowls
- loaf tin
- baking parchment
- spatula
- spoon

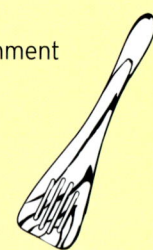

DRINKS

PINK LEMONADE

There is nothing more refreshing than a cool glass of home-made lemonade. Pink lemonade was traditionally dyed with a little beetroot juice, but this recipe uses cranberry juice for flavour and colour.

Serves 5

15 mins Prep

1

Using a potato peeler, peel the zest from the lemons, leaving as much of the white pith on the lemons as possible. Squeeze the juice from the lemons.

2

Pour the lemon juice into a large heatproof jug, and add the sugar and lemon zest. Pour over 600ml (1 pint) boiling water and stir until the sugar has dissolved.

3

Leave to cool. Then, strain the lemonade into a serving jug.

4

Stir in the cranberry juice and 200ml (7fl oz) chilled water. Sweeten with extra sugar, if desired, and serve in glasses with ice and a slice of lemon.

INGREDIENTS

- 4 unwaxed lemons
- 100g (3½oz) caster sugar
- 200ml (7fl oz) cranberry juice, chilled
- ice and lemon slices, to serve

TOOLS

- potato peeler
- knife
- chopping board
- wooden spoon
- heatproof jug
- mini sieve
- serving jug

TOP TIP

You can also add pomegranate juice to get a beautiful pink colour.

FRUIT SMOOTHIES

Smoothies are great fun to make and drink. You can create lots of variations by using different fruit or by adding rolled oats to make your drink a bit thicker.

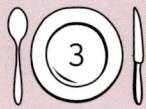

Banana and mango smoothie

INGREDIENTS

- 175ml (6fl oz) milk
- 120ml (4fl oz) plain yogurt
- 2 small bananas, sliced
- 1 small mango, roughly chopped

TOOLS

- chopping board, sharp knife, electric blender, glasses for smoothies

METHOD

- Follow the steps for the blueberry smoothie.

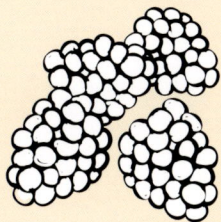

Peach and berry smoothie

INGREDIENTS

- 120ml (4fl oz) milk
- 120ml (4fl oz) plain yogurt
- 2 peaches, sliced
- 75g (2½oz) raspberries
- 75g (2½oz) strawberries, hulled
- 1 tbsp rolled oats

TOOLS

- chopping board, sharp knife, electric blender, glasses for smoothies

METHOD

- Follow the steps for the blueberry smoothie.

Blueberry, orange, and strawberry smoothie

INGREDIENTS

- 120ml (4fl oz) smooth orange juice
- 120ml (4fl oz) milk
- 120ml (4fl oz) plain yogurt
- 150g (5½oz) blueberries
- 150g (5½oz) strawberries, hulled
- 3 tbsp rolled oats
- ½ tsp vanilla extract (optional)

TOOLS

- chopping board, sharp knife, electric blender, glasses for smoothies

METHOD

- Put all the ingredients into a blender and run it on medium to high speed until everything is well mixed and smooth.
- Pour the smoothie into three glasses and serve it to your family or friends.
- Drink straight away or you'll need to stir your smoothie as it will thicken and it can separate.

HOT CHOCOLATE

This simple recipe uses good quality chocolate instead of drinking chocolate – the taste is so much better!

Serves 4 | Prep 5 mins | Cook 4 mins

INGREDIENTS

- 100g (3½oz) good quality plain, milk, or white chocolate
- 600ml (1 pint) milk
- a few drops of mint, orange, or vanilla extract
- 12 marshmallows
- cocoa powder, for dusting

TOOLS

- grater
- whisk
- saucepan

DID YOU KNOW?

Chocolate is made from cocoa beans, the seeds of cocao tree that grows in tropical rainforest.

1 Coarsely grate the chocolate. Place the milk and chocolate in a saucepan and whisk over moderate heat for 3–4 minutes until the chocolate has dissolved.

2 Add a few drops of the flavouring. Pour the hot chocolate into 4 mugs and top each with 3 marshmallows. Dust with the cocoa powder.

MILKSHAKE

Make your own delicious milkshakes with fresh fruit. This simple drink is healthy and full of natural goodness.

INGREDIENTS

- 400g (14oz) fresh strawberries or 4 bananas
- 600ml (1 pint) cold milk
- 8 scoops vanilla ice cream

TOOLS

- knife
- chopping board
- blender

1

Remove the stalks from the strawberries or peel and chop the banana. Place in a liquidizer or blender and whizz to a purée.

2

Add the milk and ice cream and blend for 1 minute until frothy. Pour into 4 tall glasses and serve. For the banana shake, try adding 4 tablespoons of toffee sauce (see step 2, page 62) or try chocolate ice cream instead of vanilla.

FOUR WAYS WITH DRINKS

Try these healthy, colourful, and easy-to-make drinks!

1

ALMOND, CASHEW, & SAFFRON MILK

If you like nuts, you will love this creamy and refreshing drink. It goes best with Indian foods.

INGREDIENTS

- 750ml (1¼ pints) milk
- 1 tsp saffron strands
- 20g (¾oz) almonds, flaked
- 45g (1½oz) cashews
- ½ tsp cardamom, ground
- 85g (3oz) honey
- 8 ice cubes

METHOD

- Heat 4 tablespoons of the milk. Soak the saffron threads in the hot milk for 15 minutes.

- Blend the saffron milk with the almonds, cashews, remaining milk, cardamom, and honey for 1–2 minutes until creamy. Chill in the refrigerator for at least 3 hours or overnight.

- Serve chilled over ice cubes.

2

MANGO-APPLE SPARKLER

This pretty sparkling drink can be made in a few seconds. Don't forget a colourful straw!

INGREDIENTS

- 115g (4oz) mango purée
- 120ml (4fl oz) apple juice
- crushed ice
- 500ml (16fl oz) soda, chilled
- 8-10 mint leaves

METHOD

- Place the mango purée, apple juice, and crushed ice in a tall glass.

- Add soda to fill. Garnish with mint leaves.

MAKE YOUR OWN

Drinks can be made in advance and kept chilled in the fridge until served. You can also try these ingredients to create more varieties of drinks.

Apples

Strawberries

Bananas

Blueberries

Orange

3

CHERRY CORDIAL

Make this cordial with chilled sparkling water and ice for a refreshing drink.

INGREDIENTS

- 1kg (2¼lb) fresh red cherries
- 600ml (1 pint) cold water
- 350g (12oz) caster sugar
- chilled still or sparkling water and ice, to serve

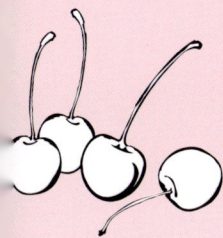

METHOD

- Cut each cherry in half and remove the stone. Place them in a pan with the cold water.

- Bring to the boil and simmer over a gentle heat for about 15 minutes until the fruit has softened. Leave to cool for 10 minutes, then place in a food processor and blend. (You may need to do this in batches.)

- Strain through a sieve into a clean pan, pressing the pulp left in the sieve. Add the sugar and, over a low heat, stir until dissolved.

- Simmer for 5 minutes. Pour into sterilized jars and store in a cool place. Pour a little of the cordial into a glass and top with chilled water and ice.

4

WATERMELON PUNCH

This pretty red punch, made from watermelon and raspberries, is perfect for a party.

INGREDIENTS

- 1 small watermelon
- 300g (10oz) fresh raspberries, plus more to serve
- 1 orange, sliced
- 20 mint leaves
- 20 ice cubes

METHOD

- Cut the watermelon in half, then cut into wedges and remove the skin.

- Cut the flesh into chunks – you need about 1kg (2¼lb). Place in a blender with the raspberries and blend until liquified.

- Strain the mixture through a sieve over a bowl. Pour into a jug or punch bowl and add the orange slices, mint, and ice cubes. Add the extra raspberries and serve immediately.

143

⭐ INDEX

SHAHI TUKDA

Crisp, golden-brown bread triangles, soaked in a creamy milk mixture, this rich dessert is sure to be the centre of attraction after a meal.

Serves 4 · Prep 4hrs 15mins · Cook 60 mins

INGREDIENTS

- 240ml (8fl oz) milk
- 4 tbsp condensed milk
- pinch of saffron
- ½ tsp ground cardamom seeds
- 2-3 drops rose essence
- 4 slices white bread
- *ghee* or vegetable oil, for frying
- 30g (1oz) blanched almonds, chopped
- 1 tbsp chopped pistachios

TOOLS

- boiling pan
- wooden spatula
- spoon
- knife
- frying pan
- slotted spoon
- kitchen towel

1

Boil the milk with the condensed milk, saffron, and cardamom until the mixture is reduced by half, stirring continuously.

2

Add the rose essence and remove from heat. Allow to cool to room temperature. Refrigerate for at least 4 hours or overnight.

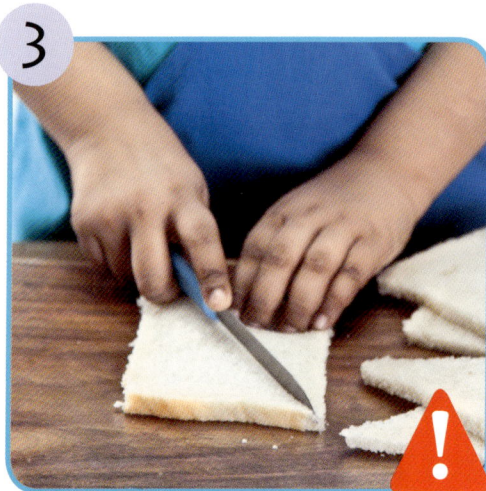

3

Cut the crusts off the bread and cut the slices diagonally. Ask an adult to help you with this step.

4

Heat the *ghee* or oil in a frying pan over medium-high heat. Fry the bread until crisp and golden. Using a slotted spoon, remove the bread from the frying pan, and drain the excess oil on a kitchen towel.